Few men have encountered the variety of faith healing experiences which real estate-dealer-turned-writer Karl Roebling met on his 10,000 mile tour. Sample these quotes from his eye-opening report . . .

"This man was injured in the eyes . . . a neighbor had blinded the man's dog . . . they had to kill it . . . he complained . . . the neighbor shot acid into his eyes . . . healed . . . now has 20/20 vision."

"Haven't spent a dime on medicine since I was saved, and no one in our church has medical treatment."

"LUNG HEALING going on. Breathe deeply . . . breathe deeply. There is a lung healing in the audience. That's right . . . breathe deeply . . . SOMEONE has received a brand-new physical heart while I'm speaking."

"Today I believe we are witnessing something never seen before. Not one revival, not one stream, not one flowing river, not one movement, but a dozen . . . . "

KARL ROEBLING is a Georgia-raised Princeton man who has been a successful copywriter for a number of years. IS THERE HEALING POWER? is his first book.

After five years in advertising agencies, he entered the land development and building business in Florida. Now, in his adopted California, he carries on his own busy practice of copywriting and promotion.

In the summer of 1971, he visited the Kathryn Kuhlman meeting he describes here. "That was a turning point," he claims. That was what set him out on the healing odyssey that took him from the Mexican border to Seattle to Denver and back home to Anaheim.

From the pages of dozens of spiral notebooks he took with him, we get this layman's eye view of the charismatic movement in America.

KARL ROEBLING

IS THERE HEALING POWER?

ONE MAN'S LOOK AT AMERICA'S FAITH HEALERS

Keats Publishing Inc. New Canaan, Connecticut

Printed by Keats Publishing, Inc.
for David C. Cook Publishing Co.

Printed in the United States of America
Library of Congress Catalog Card Number: 72-83072
ISBN 0-912692-09-X

CONTENTS

CONTENTS

WHY DID I WRITE A BOOK ABOUT HEALING?

I had heard it all my life.

"No, Karl! You know it isn't real."

"They don't really heal."

"It can't possibly be true."

"Yes, God heals, but not that way."

As a boy in Georgia, I had heard it from those I respected—teachers, doctors, writers. As I grew I heard it from friends. With a laugh or a shake of the head they easily dismissed the idea that God heals men in any other way than "natural" means or medicine.

But it wasn't that easy for me. I had a keen interest in spiritual healing taking place throughout the pages of recorded history. I had heard about men such as Oral Roberts. I had read a book by Emily Gardiner Neal. I had seen the newspaper announcements and read the reports and knew that in my adopted California, thousands of men and women believed that God healed.

I had been in the building business in Florida for some years before I moved to California and had invested in land. So I sold a piece of property, put the cash in the bank, and set forth.

For several months I drove north, east, south and west. I visited every meeting, talked to every person, read every book and story I could find that would tell me about healing. I examined the evidence for myself.

In these pages I've recorded a portion of what I saw, heard, read and thought. Travel with me on this exciting expedition.

CHAPTER 1

KATHRYN KUHLMAN—NOW NUMBER ONE

THE DOORS TO THE HUGE Shrine Auditorium in Los Angeles opened at one p.m. At one-thirty about a hundred people still waited to get in, and ushers were leading a handful at a time to find the few vacant seats among the 7,000.

By 1:55 p.m. we had balcony seats way down on one side, giving us a perfect view of the mammoth stage as well as the audience. This was a sedate fiftyish group, with a good representation of children among them.

A daytime television atmosphere pervaded, but an expectancy and a sense of spiritual communication overrode the show business feel. It was a "you're a brother . . . a smile for you . . . we're in this together" type of thing. Kathryn Kuhlman's monthly healing meeting in Los Angeles had begun.

It was a new experience for me, but, yes, I liked it. So I relaxed and turned my attention toward the platform.

The stage itself was of grand opera proportions. Ramps on both sides and in the middle ran up to it from the audience, spotlights lighted the entire area and a 300-voice choir in light orange and raspberry robes stood nine rows deep at the back.

Front and center stood the focal point of it all—Kathryn Kuhlman. No one could doubt who was the emcee. She was the only one in white . . . quick as a small bird, effortless . . . no retiring violet here.

An addict, many years on dope, stood beside her. He had been healed a month ago at one of these meetings and was here to tell about it. And tell he did. No doubt about it. He was not only healed, he was regenerated.

Then Miss Kuhlman announced that six deputy sheriffs who had sponsored the addict in the healing service the month before were in the audience. After about six calls they gathered on the stage. The addict testified and shook hands and hugged each sheriff in turn.

During this time the huge theater organ played, sometimes softly, sometimes loudly, to emphasize a point or a moment.

When the choir sang, "Oh, it's real," she called for the audience to join in. And they did. "OH . . . IT'S REAL . . . IT'S REAL . . ."

The next one she turned to told a story of nine years in a wheel chair with MS. He had been healed at a meeting in Portland, Ore., and, according to Miss Kuhlman, it had "shaken the medical profession . . . will make medical journals . . . .

"But I have nothing to do with it," she protested. When she saw him she had said, "I guess I'll give you a double dose of the Holy Spirit."

That was a month ago. Now he was healed, walking, standing, talking, and praising God.

One thing I had to get used to. Miss Kuhlman often lays on hands before a healing or when she feels it isn't quite complete or to impart a blessing. When she does, the effect is often a stunning knockout. People fall over in a faint or a slump or, in the case of the ex-addict, nearly loop the loop. He had flipped on to the floor at an accidental touch by Miss Kuhlman. After about three such falls, she laughingly warned him, "Stay away from me."

I found it hard to take at first but quite natural after I had watched it for awhile. Soon I expected it.

An usher steps behind each person to whom Miss Kuhlman is talking and gently takes him under the arms in case he falls board-straight backwards or slumps. For some it's wham! Others go limp. Some stay down awhile but others are not completely out. Meanwhile Kathryn continues the action on stage, often stepping over or around the prostrate.

When she called the MS man's wife to the platform, the audience clapped. Miss Kuhlman tried to speak but, overcome with emotion, stepped back from the microphone and covered her face with her hands. It happened several times. Her stage motions expressed her thoughts.

Was it all part of a human plan made beforehand, I wondered? No! The people were scheduled, but the emotions, I believed, were real.

Some time ago, soon after her husband was healed, Mrs. MS had made a request of Miss Kuhlman. They had been married with Mr. MS in a wheelchair, and she had never seen her husband walk before they were married. Now, she wondered, would Miss Kuhlman marry them for the second time?

Yes, she would. Right now. This time with hubby standing up.

The wheelchair had been wheeled out as a symbol. Mr. MS hadn't needed it. He was a little rusty, perhaps, as he came up the ramp, but after all, Miss Kuhlman had said, there were "muscles in that body that hadn't been used for nine years."

Miss Kuhlman was weeping openly and both smiling and crying. "This is what I live for. This is what I live for, friends. This is what I live for. I just want to be so very careful to give You the praise."

11

The theater organ played while the simple vows began. ". . . do you take this man . . ." Again she was unable to go on for a moment. Then that sparkling wit of hers broke through, "Which one of us is taking these vows?" The audience laughed with those on the stage in a natural and happy scene.

Finally she called for the wedding march, and as the happy couple walked off down the central ramp, the wheelchair was pushed off to the right—gone for good.

Was this a show? Yes, it was a show. It would be hard to top. But then it was not a "show." It was the real thing. Or was it?

The evangelist's voice broke into my thoughts. "How can I talk about an offering after that?" she cried.

I couldn't believe my ears. What an inappropriate time. Why *do* preachers do this?

"If anyone can withhold from Him after that," she was saying. "Don't take your two eyes for granted . . . Don't take your lips for granted . . . no, don't take them for granted . . .

"Give, give, GIVE, Give nothing less than the best."

I thought I'd like to give but not under a wave of emotion. Was I built up deliberately for that? (Later in the meeting I felt the sincerity of the appeal for funds.)

Onto the stage came an aged man who had been given one week to live because of cancer. In a halting voice he explained that he had been wheelchair ridden, had nearly died but had been healed at a meeting last month.

Miss Kuhlman spoke to him. "Raise that leg. Raise it higher. Higher! Now the other one. Raise it higher."

To the audience she said something to the effect that when it's God's work, we don't have to worry about putting it to the test.

"Now, run. Run!

"Faster!"

He ran across the stage.

"Now, run back."

He was a spry old fellow.

Kathryn turned to the friend who had brought the aged man to the healing service and—zap. He was out.

To the aged man she said, "There! Now *you* can help *him* up," and the audience laughed with her.

As attendants began to push the man's wheelchair off, she cried, "No, no! Bring that back." Following her instructions, they helped the zapped friend into the wheelchair, and she said to the old man, "There, now you can push your friend."

And he went off center stage and down the ramp to the applause and cheers of the crowd.

She spoke next about the Jesus movement. "I believe in the WONDERFUL JESUS, Son of God . . . and a lot of Protestant ministers would do well to get in and join the Jesus movement.

"I believe Jesus heals. And if that's the Jesus movement, I'm behind it and for it."

She stood center stage at the microphone, about three steps back from it, striving for complete attention from the audience.

"I pray that not one will seek Kathryn Kuhlman . . . I cannot use the Holy Spirit. He uses the vessel . . . ."

She spoke of healings. "Peter and John went up together into the temple . . . And a certain man lame from his mother's womb . . . Who seeing Peter and John . . . asked an alms. And Peter, fastening his eyes upon him . . . said . . . Silver and gold have I none; but such as I have give I thee: In the name of Jesus Christ of Nazareth rise up and walk" (Acts 3: 1-6).

Her delivery was spontaneous—no notes. She would approach the microphone, then back off as she let her voice—incredibly deep at one moment and bird-like at

13

another—range with her feelings. There was no doubt she felt what she said.

Next she talked about the perfect tree that was complete. "Then the PALMERWORM . . ." Her voice rang out as she repeated passages from Joel. "That which the palmerworm hath left hath the locust eaten; and that which the locust left hath the cankerworm eaten; and that which the cankerworm hath left hath the caterpiller eaten."

"The CANKERWORM," she cried so that it could be heard across the street. The seats rattled and minds rattled and the audience paid closer attention.

She was trying to say something and the cankerworm was only the thread, the framework of her message. She seemed to be listening for something else. This was no ordinary sermon. The preaching was about to be done by something, someone else, something or someone she was aware of but we weren't. We heard and saw only the story about the Church.

"That CANKERWORM!"

Such a deep voice! Such volume! And now, without doubt, she had their attention.

" . . . some of the gifts no longer in evidence.

" . . . fewer great miracle services now.

" . . . leaves begin to fall."

She taught that the leaves or fruits began to come off the tree that had been perfectly filled out and furnished. As she warmed to her task, she also took time to remark, "Any Christian religion or theology that denies the blood of Jesus Christ is not Christian but anti-Christian."

Then she returned to her main theme. "I will restore the years the locust hath eaten, and that great time of restoration is NOW.

"Things are happening today that could not have happened five, ten or fifteen years ago . . . Look up . . . if you have spiritual eyesight. Look . . . all of the

14

gifts . . . restored to the Church . . . we are living in those last days now . . . ."

She quoted again from Joel, "I will POUR out my spirit . . . prophesy . . . your young men shall see visions . . . ."

The hippie beside me was in a trance, his hands turned palms upward on his lap, his eyes closed, his face up. "Ey, Lord," he repeated.

Then she began an earnest and plaintive appeal to God that surpassed anything she had exhibited before. She stood about two steps from the microphone, turned about sixty degrees from it. Her hands were up in the air and her voice cried out.

"Please don't take my life from me. Please don't take my life. I want to see it through to the finish." I got the feeling she meant this healing work—the healing of all the world, the end of suffering.

She cried again, this time from fresh depths of earnestness, yes, loneliness. "So long I've felt that I've been standing alone in it . . .

"Trust me, please . . . I will never betray the trust You put in me."

She was crying.

"Jesus will forgive your sins . . . Jesus will give you a new purpose . . . SON of the LIVING GOD . . .

"LUNG HEALING going on. Breathe deeply . . . breathe deeply. There is a lung healing in the audience. That's right . . . breathe deeply.

"SOMEone has received a brand-new physical heart while I'm speaking."

At this point she recited at least twenty, perhaps twenty-five specific healings that she saw or felt in the audience. I was amazed and stunned and missed most of the notes. What I did get read . . .

"Cataract . . .

"Stomach healing . . .

"Second stomach healing . . . ulcer . . . the burning

15

has left . . .

"Take that hearing aid out, please." Earlier she had noted the healing of the ear and now was following it up.

The audience was relatively quiet when the first healing came. Then there were moans and gasps of joy from somewhere to the right below me. The crowd stirred as different areas became aware of a recipient in their midst.

"That person with cancer . . . STAND UP . . . begin walking."

To another, "Take off that brace. You've been completely healed.

"Bone fracture . . . completely healed.

"Arthritis of the feet . . . all that arthritis has gone . . . stomp down on that foot."

She was happy, smiling, moving around, in total command.

"Arthritis of the shoulder . . . raise that arm . . . that arm has completely loosened." This was the first one from the choir.

Then they began coming up on the platform. They came up the ramps and lined up behind a man at a microphone about fifty feet from the center of the stage. He had first announced the healing of the arthritic shoulder and she had repeated it. Now he announced, "Cancer of the lymph gland."

Miss Kuhlman turned her attention from the audience, where the initial flush of healings had dropped off, to the stage where the healed were coming and lining up. There were fifty or sixty at that point in lines on both sides of the stage.

When she turns her attention to those on the stage, I learned, it means that people will drop like cord wood from her loving touch to the temples. Friends, patients past, patients today, anyone close by who might receive a blessing from her hands—they all fall.

16

The man's voice came over the speaker, "Cancer of the lung . . . feels the Lord has healed him of cancer of the lung."

By that time it was 4:30 p.m. The meeting had been going on for three-and-a-half hours and quite a few people had gone. There were still many on the stage, however, in those two lines.

We got up to leave and were close to the outside exit doors when we heard a scream from the auditorium and a cry from the audience. We ran back in time to hear Miss Kuhlman say, "Come on! Come on! Walk!"

She stood center left on the stage and a little tiger in cowboy clothes, about four years old, stood at the right. The little guy had just had his brace removed and Miss Kuhlman was urging him to walk. But he wasn't about to, and he let everyone know it with another mighty scream. (The first scream sounded like the devil coming out of him. It was unearthly, unlike anything I'd ever heard before, and it had electrified the audience.)

Now Miss Kuhlman insisted that he walk. No one was within five feet of him. Someone near him held his brace, and he was in the spotlight. But he still wouldn't move.

She stayed with it with the greatest combination of love and command I've ever heard. She didn't coax. She told him; she ordered—yet she really didn't order. She loved him. That was it. She led him—and she never wavered.

She talked to something in him that I wasn't aware of nor was he. But Miss Kuhlman saw it and knew it and addressed herself to it. If she had been talking to the little boy as he saw himself, she would have given up.

"Come on! Walk! Come on! Walk!"

I felt that the audience had begun to waver, but not

17

Miss Kuhlman. She was as bright as ever.

Well, here's one she'll lose, I thought. He had started to move but stopped, and I felt he couldn't be roused.

Just as brightly as though she were greeting a neighbor in the morning she spoke, "Come on!" Her voice had bells in it. It sang. "Come on! Walk!"

Now the boy's father had gone to the other side of the stage and she said, "Go to Daddy. Run! Run to Daddy. Run! Run," and he took off like a rocket.

The audience went wild. They cheered and clapped. They weren't just spectators. They were a part of it. Their hearts were on the line.

That didn't satisfy Kathryn Kuhlman. No. Back to Daddy the child went . . . back and forth. Now he's free. He can run. He's healed and he knows it. He's out of that brace forever.

Ten minutes later we were still working our car out of the lot. It was five o'clock, and I don't know how long the meeting went on.

CHAPTER 2

ORAL ROBERTS—THE FORMER
NUMBER ONE

TULSA, I HAD HEARD, was the home of Oral Roberts University, and a passerby confirmed that when I inquired.

"Yes," she said, somewhat defensively. "It's a really beautiful place."

I found it just outside of town. No tent. A multi-million dollar investment instead, from the beautiful gates and winding road to the dominant point of the campus—the prayer tower.

To the receptionist at the university center I stated my mission: "I'm writing a book about healing. Isn't this place all built on spiritual healing?"

"Yes," she said.

Slowly I put the pieces together. The former number one is out of the healing business himself. A number of years ago he closed down his last tent. In 1965 he opened a university. In 1968 he joined the Methodist church. Now he travels, speaks, preaches Christ, puts on TV Specials. The healing is handled by others.

Roberts, a university spokesman told me, "began in Enid, Okla., where he felt God told him to rent a hall and go ahead with a healing ministry. He did—he stepped forth, rented a hall, and announced that there would be prayers given for the sick. He was immediately swamped with applicants and his healing ministry was born.

"The whole thrust of his ministry is spiritual healing through the power of God by the laying on of hands and releasing of (the patient's) faith. You can read about it all in his book MY TWENTY YEARS OF A MIRACLE MINISTRY."

"This university is an extension of his shadow.

"Oral Roberts is well-loved in this community. He is accepted by all in Tulsa—Jew, Catholic . . . of course, he has had an economic impact on the community . . . he is a director of National Bank of Tulsa. . . ."

The spokesman continued in his fast-moving, definitive way.

"Oral Roberts is an evangelist, dreamer, goal-setter . . ."

"Is he Doctor Roberts, Reverend, or what?" I asked.

"President or Reverend—not Doctor. I'm not sure he ever finished college."

I also learned that Oral Roberts University had a special library collection of books on Pentecostalism, and I met the guardian of the Pentecostal Room, Miss Walker. The room wasn't open in the summer, she informed me, but could be opened specially. In the winter it was open with an attendant.

Miss Walker discussed healing. She spoke of ". . . emotionalism . . . momentary healing . . . those who can't *keep* the healing. . ." She was not referring to the Oral Roberts Crusades, which obviously she felt were solid. But this phenomenon of not being able to keep the healing, she was willing to deal with directly.

"People say they (the ones who can't keep it) are hypnotized. They're not hypnotized . . . They get the healing but you have got to stand on it . . . got to stand on the Word . . . you'll get rebuttal from the enemy . . . the enemy will bring the symptoms back. . . ."

I began to note in this and other discussions that God was not regarded as having sent the illness. I got the impression from what she told me that Oral Roberts would rather have for healing only those to whom the Word had been preached. Faith comes through "hearing of the word"—faith being necessary to the healing.

She spoke of forgiving. I believe she was giving me a healing treatment—at any rate a good look-through. I felt pretty transparent and thought this lady ought to be in healing work.

She went on, speaking now of God, "He'll heal the non-saved quicker."

I questioned.

"Yes, He'll sometimes heal the non-saved or non-Christian or baby Christian sooner than the saved non-forgiving."

That made sense. The saved non-forgiving had to come before Him without anything against his brother. She quoted Scripture, and it seemed to me she knew what she was talking about.

Miss Walker pointed out several other things to me. "They call it divine healing, not spiritual . . . meaning God coming in on the scene to heal. . ." If she healed me she'd be "just a channel." She explained it would be her "hands in place of His hands."

She told of the Day of Pentecost in the Book of Acts. Of the Comforter ". . . another Person . . . Holy Ghost whom the Father sends in Jesus' name." We become "imbued with power and filled with the Holy Ghost TO OVERFLOWING." She emphasized the latter and said that I was not yet filled with the Holy Ghost.

I learned that the healer could have moments of being filled to overflowing when persons were healed, then walk out on the sidewalk and not necessarily heal. The influence could come and go.

However, it was clear that the influence more easily came and went through someone cleansed completely of all impediment (such as lack of forgiveness) and through someone who had been filled to overflowing with the Holy Ghost.

Miss Walker was preparing to go home for the night. It was 4:30 p.m. but the library stayed open until 9:30 p.m. "We have hundreds of researchers come here. Many from Europe," she said. "Stay and read. You may read at any of the desks. But be *sure* to leave before 9:30 p.m.," she said with a smile.

It wasn't until a month or so later back in California that I met Rev. Robert DeWeese, traveling from Tulsa on behalf of the Oral Roberts' organization, holding what they call "Partners' Meetings." A meeting was scheduled in a theater in the Municipal Auditorium in San Jose.

The exact nature of that meeting I was to discover slowly. No advertisements. One small sign at the door. About 250 in a room seating 450. A partners' meeting.

The lights were just going off as I arrived and a film was beginning. It was an Oral Roberts' film of a world-wide tour of a group of young people.

This whole organization expresses love and outgoingness. There's a good spirit there. I'm at home around the Roberts' organization. I don't feel them arguing with me doctrinally. I feel they're willing to accept me if the Holy Spirit is willing to accept me. The movie gave me that feeling.

The young people themselves were talking.

". . . give them something that will change their lives."

This was something I was beginning to hear more and more of . . . change lives . . . that there was no contact with the real thing without a life-change. These changes bring us out. We become more sharply etched, more in focus, more aware of what we are, of what we need to change and *aren't*.

Lights. Oh, there was that social-director thing I had met in other places. I *will* be drawn in, I said to myself, steeling myself so I would jump in. Because once I did it, it was fun.

The stage was sparse—no decorations, no band, no organ, no piano. Just a podium and a speaker, backdrop and sidedrops. No singers, no costumes, etc.

DeWeese came out, and someone distributed registration cards.

". . . prayer is just a wonderful experience . . ." DeWeese began. ". . . had 300 people in Las Vegas in the middle of a storm . . . dust, rain . . . After here we go to Portland . . ."

I guess he's about 50—turned out he was older. Dressed in a blue double-breasted blazer, pink shirt, blue-red striped tie, gray trousers. Gray hair, tan dark-rim glasses—very conservative.

DeWeese began recounting his own life and experience and I really liked the approach. For one thing the "you ought to" approach is a pretty hard way to go today. People want to hear the experiences of others and make up their own minds.

"Will you take Jesus Christ with you every where you go?" This was the question to which, in his late teens, he had replied, "yes." He went on to become the Southern California record-holder in some track event—sprints or hurdles or the like. Then the call came that astounded him—the call to "give it up." He answered "yes" to that too—though he didn't know why.

This special call that he received to drop athletics presented a conflict in his mind—and still does today. He brought out his admiration for the Oral Roberts University sports program and told of a basketball game in which the star ORU player was injured: "Brother Roberts followed him into the dressing room, prayed for him, healed him and he came back and won. The opposing coach said, 'I knew I'd have to play five players but not the Lord, too.' "

After more stories DeWeese began to pray. "Everybody needs healing in his body . . . nobody's perfect . . . The law of the spirit of life in Christ Jesus . . . James said pray ye for one another that ye may be healed . . . got four nice healings on this . . . deaf. . . ." He was talking so fast I couldn't get it.

"Jewish lady—healed of gangrenous leg that was to be cut off next week in New York . . . Best miracle on this trip was God opened the eyes of a little girl in Atlanta . . ." He was talking of healings on Roberts' crusades in the past.

"I'll close the service with a prayer line . . ."

It slowly dawned. These people were part of the Roberts' organization in a sense. The meeting was about half-way between public and private, with a congregation that was about half-way between direct organization members and private citizens.

These were people who were in some way contributing regularly to the Roberts' operation, who loved Brother Roberts and who had received, as I could see it, some real benefit from Roberts, his books, his prayers and his ministers such as DeWeese. Offhand, I would say, most were here because of healing of some sort. I wouldn't have been surprised to learn that half the people here had had hands laid on by Brother Roberts in crusades in California.

If not directly, most if not all had felt the touch or the contact through some form of his contact-outreach. For this is the name of his game: the point of contact. It works. Ask the army that follows him. On any given day, were Brother Roberts to ask for letters from those healed, the purpose of those letters to convince some unbeliever standing beside him, within a week I do not believe you would be able to see the unbeliever for the mountain of mail were it to be wafted down upon him.

Ask the man who owns one, the old ad used to read. Well, ask the man who's been healed spiritually. You're liable not to be able to turn him off.

DeWeese: "I'll lay on hands . . . I hold 150 meetings a year . . . up to 1,500 people (per meeting) . . . We're missionaries, you know . . . to us, it's just a privilege . . . God calls us . . . but the costs of conversion . . . about $10 a head average conversion cost of those who come to Christ. . . ."

He spoke of foreign missions and of sacrifice, and I noted that he didn't mind pitching $50 or more. Seed offerings. Plant a seed. Release your faith. The more he talked about money, the more I realized he was talking to an inner group—people who were basically sold already.

Now he passed out free copies of the book SEED FAITH. One to a family. Hands showed need for about five more than were on hand, but he kept praying audibly for the need to be met, and copies were passed around from those who had them in the audience. Finally all had copies. This pleased everybody no end. It was a nice little demonstration of God's love, and everybody felt good.

That part over, the prayer line began.

The concept of the partners en-masse lying back of the great organization up front with a vital youth image, funding often what could not be otherwise funded, and being nurtured by this selfless, dedicated minister who must know he's in fund-raising work, startled me. I guess I just thought that all that youth image was self-generative or self-perpetuative. But back of any happy teenager is usually a hard-working daddy, a faceless mommie, a granny and a grandpop or two.

I was waking up fast to many things in this meeting,

and I woke up faster when Rev. DeWeese came down off that platform and started calling out his prayer line with *me first*. Now that sat me bolt upright. Did he see spirituality in me? No, I was just the first one on his left, farthest to the front, and thus first. "Yes, you . . . come on up."

"Now, here's what I want you to do." (Oh, why did he start with me? I'm not even a partner.)

Now we were face-to-face in front of the whole audience, and he was giving instructions as to what he wanted done. Wanted done? I was still foggy.

"You put your hand on my shoulder . . . thus . . ." He had to literally place my hand against the front of his left shoulder. He repeated himself several times . . . "and then I place my hand on your shoulder . . . and I pray for you . . . and as I pray for you, YOU PRAY FOR ME. . . ."

Then it was over and he was ministering to the others. They lined up all the way into the back. I sat now on the left-hand side of the auditorium and watched the rest of the meeting.

I heard his phrases, "My God, meet this need by Thy power. . . ." A lady told him, "two years ago God healed me of a stroke. . . ." He laid hands on all. Many were there just for the blessing. They were the faithful, and Brother DeWeese had a blessing from God and from the whole Roberts' organization.

"God meet your need . . .

"Jesus touch you tonight . . .

"Ha ha ha—felt your faith, sister . . .

(Remember, they are touching him, too.)

"You touch me; I touch you . . .

". . . that our faith go to God . . .

"In the name of Jesus who loves you . . . who died for you . . . thank You, Jesus, for Your power.

". . . who forgives our sins and heals our diseases . . . Praise God . . ."

Pastor DeWeese testified. "My wife was dying of leukemia. Doctors had given her up. Yellow jaundice . . . pernicious anemia . . . leukemia . . . thirty-two years ago I poured out my heart to God in prayer . . . God spoke to me, said, 'Now is the time . . .' I went into her bedroom—and you know, God healed her then and there. She's outside now. Speak to her . . .

"Touch the arthritis in . . ." He was ministering again.

"Two 92's . . ."

This is an older crowd.

"Practically raised from the dead . . . Isn't that wonderful. . . ."

Dear Lord, how does he do it? He was laying hands on this whole crowd—250, maybe more. That's a lot of laying on of hands. Many were there for the blessing, not the healing, and the enormous receptivity that I had seen in general meetings was not there. Some were up only or mainly for conversation. You could tell the healing ones, though. But I wondered if the preacher would be ready for real healing where there was so much general thought.

A woman testified, "My diaphragm was ruptured but was healed." Then she asked for healing of arthritis.

Someone requested prayer for Mary Daley in the hospital.

He laid hands on a girl child with a touch of monsterism problem.

"Healed in the crusade," she said, "haven't had a cold since."

"Wants healing of glaucoma and arthritis. God grant it. Amen!"

CHAPTER 3

DON STEWART—MIRACLE VALLEY, ARIZONA

DOWN FROM ALBUQUERQUE I drove, south to Las Cruces where I picked up I-10 and pointed the car toward Tucson. In Arizona my route led me south on route 80 to the Mexican border, north again to route 92 and finally to Bisbee. From there it was just a short run to my destination—Miracle Valley, Ariz.

This was dry, desert, Cochise country, broken up by 9,000 foot mountains, mining towns and, in this case, a Bible school-business-healing complex that attracts thousands to camp-style meetings.

I had first heard of Don Stewart and Miracle Valley on my car radio. I tuned in part way through a broadcast and heard patient after patient healed. Then came the announcement that I could get a certain book in exchange for a five dollar donation and that in July I could attend a gathering of friends from around the world. From the next town I wrote a check for the book and marked the date to be there.

Now from the heights I could see it—Miracle Valley with a red, green and gold dome in the distance. The road gradually lost altitude and I entered the complex through a western-style whitewashed pole-gate that bore the notice "Miracle Valley Bible College." The main building and others behind it were low ranch-type buildings of wood and masonry, with poles in place of square-sawn lumber for rafters and railings.

In the administration building I filled out a card and got a bunk assignment—no charge. Then I prepared for the chapel service at 6:00 p.m.

Miracle Valley used to be the home of A. A. Allen Revivals. Allen, one of the big names in faith healing for several years after Oral Roberts took his last tent down, had passed on about a year back, and Don Stewart was his appointed successor. MIRACLE, an attractive four-color magazine I picked up at the center, described the activities of Don Stewart and the "Compassion Explosion" crusades he was holding, as well as his itinerary, broadcast times, and stories and testimonies of healing.

On a July evening in Arizona, my notes read, some 450 people are gathered in an auditorium that would easily seat 1,500. Harold Woodson is preaching about Jesus. "Some know Him as the foundation . . . the cornerstone . . . the healer . . . the Master . . . Lord . . . messenger . . . ambassador . . . Lily of the valley . . . rose of Sharon."

Now Woodson sings, accompanied by an organ. A speaker in front and one in the rafters bellow his voice loudly. And it gets louder.

Now he's preaching about Christ again, and this time it's as loud as the singing. The man beside me appears embarrassed and mentions that this is a youth meeting.

There is that doctrine again. I've heard it in several places since I began this search. "He made you free 1900 years ago. He's not *going* to make you free . . . He's not *going* to heal you. He healed you 1,971 years ago when He stretched out between heaven and earth and said, 'Father, it is finished.' "

Now Don Stewart is on stage. He's good looking, mid-thirties, a youth image with a touch of maturity.

He's dressed in a blue jacket, dark trousers and red shirt with a red, white, and blue mottled tie.

"Say, YEAH!" The congregation does, several times.

The choir comes in across the back of the stage now, fifty voices in two rows of maroon gowns with gold collars. A row of chairs in front of the choir seats the preachers, a huge grand piano stands on the left. The big speakers are blaring, squawking, blasting the music, and we're about an hour into the service.

Up until this time I thought they'd had music. But Stewart begins to yell into the mike. "Dynamite of your resurrection. Explosion of God's dynamite to take place in your heart tonight. Let it explode." Loud, brother, loud!

A man jumps up and dances in front.

A woman in the aisle has got it—she's dancing.

Ten women out there in the aisle now.

Nobody sleeps in this service. Cobwebs that had been in my being for years are getting up and walking out. It's like a decibelic purge.

"Let that compassion explode!

"Yes, Jesus . . .

"That I might get to know Him . . ."

Wheoooo . . . loud! This vitality. This electrification. This stunning racket.

Now they're into a jazz number called, "A-men!" and it's loud. For fifteen minutes it goes on, choir swaying, like a maroon and gold sea, song leader in candy striped shirt, everybody singing. I sing like everyone else. I sing, I hallelujah, praise God, thank Jesus and do everything the others do except dance (but I feel like it).

Now another wild song. Remember boogie woogie? Some 200 people are up dancing around the room. The man beside me says, "Some people dance in the Spirit and some just dance."

It's after eight and I chat with this fellow. I have a

question, "Is it possible to be healed without 'biting the sawdust'?" He had used the term earlier for the trance or keeling over that often accompanies healing.

"Yes, you don't have to keel over to be healed."

"Can you bite the sawdust without being healed?"

"Oh, yes, it's just a blessing."

He continued speaking about baptism of the Holy Ghost. "You enter into a spiritual realm . . . usually in a different language. You *feel* the people you're praying for . . . a prayer prayed there . . . the devil can't intercept it."

"Moses' rod . . . he threw it down and it became a snake . . . Pharaoh called for his magicians . . . magician threw down his rod and it became a snake. But Moses' snake ate it up. So there's a false and a real.

"Only by baptism of the Holy Spirit can you tell the difference."

I thumb through a copy of MIRACLE and read about H. Kent Rogers, "20th Century Apostle of Faith who preaches the miracle-working word." One evening his preaching was interrupted by shouts of "I can see." Hattie Fore, a blind woman evangelist in the meeting, was suddenly able to distinguish daylight from darkness. A photo of Rogers shows him smiling and talking to four-year-old Helen Cabilao who was badly crippled but is now healed. Rogers is smiling and holding her brace.

Now Don Stewart is singing. He's no pro. He doesn't mind singing on—five minutes, seven minutes—and everytime he comes to the chorus something very beautiful comes over the audience.

"Somewhere, someplace, the devil came up behind you . . . pulled you down." He begins to preach. "A certain man went down . . . fell among thieves . . . man was living in Jerusalem . . . Holy place . . . of victory.

Bible says he went *down* to Jericho. You'll never be successful if you LEAVE JERUSALEM."

The preaching is spectacular now with Stewart all over the stage. He speaks fast, slow, loud, soft. He's dramatic, emphatic.

Now he's on his knees—"Battle between spirit and flesh."

He's up and down, back and forth across the stage. "While you're lying there." And he's down on the stage illustrating his point. "The devil's laughing at you . . . HA HA HA HA HA HA HA HA HA." He does a good imitation of a devilish laugh and repeats it three times.

"Have you left Jerusalem? . . . gone down to Jericho? . . . fallen among thieves . . . been stripped of love . . . talent . . . anointing?

"COME DOWN THESE AISLES . . ."

And they came!

"KNEEL HERE!"

Those down front kneel. Now the whole house kneels, the preachers on the platform and the choir kneel. I kneel too.

The song leader starts to sing. Stewart is on his knees, front center platform, elbows on the seat of a chair, head down in prayer.

While Stewart prays the song leader, mike on a long cord, walks around the stage singing. "Lord, is it I?" It's very loud.

"OH, LAOWAOD . . . OH . . ." It goes on ten, fifteen minutes. The traps crash, the supplicants at the front grow restless and several leave.

Who can take the noise? Many in the audience are up, swaying and raising hands. More of the supplicants leave the front while some dance. It's getting wilder and all the supplicants have left.

Woodson is up to speak. "Thank God!"

What? Is that all? No laying on of hands? No

touching temples? Not this time. The service is over.

By their own admission, the music of the Miracle Valley folks is controversial. With their permission I quote from an article, "Prophetic Music," by Rev. Jon A. Jennas from an issue of MIRACLE.

"In PROPHETIC MUSIC (The music that produces miracles) . . . always present . . . is . . . Divine Compassion. This is sometimes called, 'The Anointing' . . . You do not have to understand . . . in order to receive . . . David . . . Joshua . . . Gideon. . . . Some critical infidels have said that our music is 'a bundle of confusion.' They are probably right. PROPHETIC MUSIC is a compassionate explosion which produces the effect of confusion in the enemy's camp . . . confuses . . . devils and causes them to take their flight. . . . A young woman in Atlanta testified . . . 'While the singers and musicians were ministering, the power of God hit my mother and she leaped out of the wheelchair.' An auto accident victim testified: 'When Gene Martin began to sing, I felt the power of God in my spine. The pain left within two minutes! I jumped up and ran.' One newspaper reporter said, 'I have never before heard such music, and I have never before seen such miracles.' "

For my own part I feel that Don Stewart has a sweeter or more harmonious sense of music emanating from him than I get from the band. The sense of Presence retreated when he quit singing and preaching and knelt for fifteen minutes. Obviously, for other people, it was just the opposite.

CHAPTER 4

KENNETH HAGIN—THE QUIET BULL

I ENTERED THE KENNETH E. HAGIN Evangelistic Association's two-story brick headquarters on Utica Street in Tulsa and delivered my lead line. "I'm doing a book on spiritual healing, and someone told me this is where some of it is going on."

"You better believe it!" chirped the attractive receptionist-secretary—no disbeliever, she. She disappeared, and in a few moments returned to lead me through the offices and publishing area in back, up the stairs and into the office of Buddy Harrison.

Harrison is a smiling man, about 35, a little rotund, serious, a preacher and thinker on the one hand, relaxed, outgoing sales type on the other hand. I asked about healing and he told me about the Full Gospel Fellowship Convention being held in Tulsa beginning that very day. The concept "full gospel" includes healing.

Where is Kenneth Hagin? "Brother Hagin is in Denver this week . . . Minneapolis next. . . .

"Not *revivals* as such . . . people are religiously biased. . . we have All Faiths Crusades . . . if in a Baptist church, people think it's Baptist, if in an Assembly of God Church, they think it's Assembly of God . . . our work is INTERDENOMINATIONAL . . . we put on our own Crusades. . . ."

"Would this be Pentecostal?"

"Yes! We believe you are born into the body of Christ . . . not into a church . . . believers, not Baptists or Methodists. . . ."

The point seemed to be that the individual is a believer, and that there are "a lot of believers who are not filled with the Spirit." This would be one level of experience—a believer who is not filled with the Spirit.

However, "Pentecostal experience is a further work of the Holy Spirit. A mere believer knows the Holy Spirit and new birth but it's another experience to be filled."

He was getting at the healing phenomenon and spoke of drink of water, salvation, river, and said we should drink it more. In this way, through drinking of the rivers of the waters of salvation, we become filled—Spirit-filled.

Was it necessary to be Spirit-filled to heal? "Healing is by faith . . . Reception or transmission of healing is possible in both the Spirit-filled and non-Spirit-filled believer, but transmission is much more likely in the Spirit-filled."

Now Buddy Harrison began to warm to his task and launched into a spontaneous sermon.

Do people accept the idea of healing today better than they did ten years ago? "Not particularly," said Harrison, surprising me with his answer. But he added, "In certain areas, yes."

My observations indicated that people today generally accept the idea of spiritual healing, but that ten years ago they did not. Tulsa, however, amazed me. Here, everyone I asked believed in spiritual healing.

I asked Harrison what was the difference between the more-or-less pastoral areas where faith seemed to run so high, and cities such as New York, etc. For even in California, where belief in spiritual healing runs high, and an anything-is-possible attitude governs the land, there is general non-knowledge and even rejection of the concept in many areas.

"It's like Sodom and Gomorrah," Harrison said, ". . . certain spirits that dominated cities . . . good spirits in some areas . . . Basically the cities are controlled by evil powers."

I asked Harrison about Hagin's schedule. "Rev. Hagin is in the field . . . fields are white to harvest . . . Denver through Sunday." Today was Monday. If I was to see Hagin at all, it would have to be at Denver.

"He starts praying for the sick Tuesday . . . first two days are teaching. . . ."

This was the first mention of teaching. " . . . teaching first . . . Scriptures say . . . Jesus' procedure was first to teach . . . then preach . . . then pray for the sick. . . .

"Basically our ministry has been a teaching ministry for believers . . . Hosea 4: 6 . . . 'My people are destroyed for lack of knowledge . . .' Faith . . . gives you a knowledge of what God says . . . knowledge of certain facts . . . way to act . . . We teach salvation . . . healing . . . a complete knowledge of God as much as possible. . . ."

This teaching is integral to the healing practice, then, I gathered. Rev. Hagin taught in the mornings and conducted the healing ministry at night.

When I told Harrison I would go to Denver, he suggested that when witnesses were called for, I should volunteer and go forward to witness the healings at point blank range. It occurred to me that my disbelief might interfere—but I didn't tell Harrison. Disbelief was the last thing on his mind as he gave me the names of Rev. Hagin's two assistants and told me to contact them beforehand to be sure I was a witness.

Harrison said, speaking now of Hagin, "When anointing comes on him, he receives one of the nine gifts of the Spirit mentioned in I Corinthians 12. The nine gifts operate as the Spirit of God wills."

Recipients of the healing by Brother Hagin fall over in the manner I described earlier. Harrison said that Hagin touches their foreheads with the flat of his hand, pushing lightly against them and they go out. He noted that this was not another system, apparently used by some, which bends the head backwards and causes fainting.

I asked if they had a church for which they recruited members through the crusades. No! Furthermore, one could get on the Hagin mailing list only by asking to do so. The organization has people who support it regularly. It was incorporated in 1963 in Garland, Tex. In 1966 Buddy Harrison joined. At that time the mailing list had only 250 names, the organization owned one typewriter and had one book published.

Harrison went out on crusades with Hagin and worked the platform. Now the list is 11,000 names—and it could be much bigger except for the above-mentioned requirement and the policy of keeping "only those we're helping." They also broadcast on 37 radio stations and have three closed-circuit TV tapes. Their goal is fifty radio stations this year, 250 in two to three years, then television.

The whole thing is based on healing? "No . . . had quit praying for the sick," Buddy Harrison answered. I registered surprise.

The ministry had begun with healing I learned, then had gone to "strictly teaching." In the beginning, God had told Rev. Hagin that "he had a healing ministry." He began healing. Then he got away from healing and stressed strictly teaching. He built up his teaching materials. He built up his staff.

Harrison explained the need for staff this way, "You can't get under the anointing and take care of details . . . it's the supernatural and the natural."

Someone must "lead songs, take up offerings, sell books . . . do detail work."

Now the ministry is "going back toward the healing ministry." "In September, 1970 . . . at a Full Gospel Businessmen's meeting . . . teaching . . . Lord confronted him about healing ministry . . . he started healing again. . . .

"God uses the healing ministry to draw attention to *Him*, not the *man* . . .

" . . . Omnipotent God decides when and where . . . there's no church board to pass it . . . By putting emphasis on the healing . . . more people are saved by healing than by evangelistic message. . . ." and he cited figures.

"God had told him, get your messages in book form, tapes, etc. . . . don't preach, *TEACH*. . . ."

Why? "You can get healed . . . slain in spirit . . . yet enemy can steal your healing . . . How to *hang* on to what you've received. . . . 'Resist the devil, and he will flee from you' (James) . . . 'neither give place to the devil' . . .

"Jesus . . . resisting Satan . . . said, 'it is written.'

"If he hadn't known what was written . . . couldn't have resisted the temptations . . .

"You have to resist the devil . . . God doesn't . . . Jesus has already whipped him . . . went into the pits of hell . . . conquered . . . rose triumphant . . .

"It's as if someone unknown to you deposited $1,000 in your bank account . . . when you find out about it, you can use it . . . Jesus deposited in our spiritual account. . . . We don't *have* to go to hell. He's done it. . . . By His stripes . . . . Because He's suffered we don't. . . .

"He has deposited already ALL. . . ."

Buddy cited also Ephesians 1: 3.

"All we've got to do is write the check . . .

"Salvation . . . healing . . .

38

"Jesus did a COMPLETE *work* . . . not a matter of God doing anything else . . . People say God's going to heal you . . . God's not *going* to, He's done *done* it . . . But until you know He's done it, you can't act on it."

I said then something to this effect: that healing had passed from phenomenon to how to do it—to YOU can do it.

Buddy Harrison spoke out immediately, "Mark 16: 16-18—These signs shall follow . . . five signs . . . If they're not following you there's a reason . . . you don't believe, don't know. . . ."

My thoughts kept running. How could this have happened, this revolution in healing, in outlook toward divine healing, in concepts of teaching it—that it can be taught—without the world generally knowing it?

I went immediately to Denver where I attended a Kenneth L. Hagin Evangelistic meeting in an Assemblies of God chapel in a residential section. By seven p.m. about half of the 400 wooden folding chairs were taken—first rows first. This was a young audience, nicely dressed, white collar.

A most cheerful man of about 60 greeted me, "Bless you, Brother."

I sat near the aisle on the right-hand side of the auditorium, third row. Here I had a clear view of the area just in front of the speaker's rostrum—the area where I expected healings would take place. These I wanted to see.

I took out my sketch pen and tablet and began making sketch notes. A young man appeared over my right shoulder. "Do you sketch a lot, Sir?" "Yes," I replied, somewhat startled. "Praise the Lord," he said enthusiastically and departed.

There were six people at the rail at the front of the church, praying. From time to time others came up and some left. Reverend Hickey, the pastor of the

39

church, came out with a song leader and the meeting began.

"Ah, Jesus!" "Hallelujah!" Voices in front and back and to the side.

"O Magnify the Lord with me . . . Blessed Lamb of God . . . Jesus gives us Vic-to-ry . . ." Everyone sang and clapped and began having a good time.

After five or seven minutes of singing, the song leader hawked the books, tapes, cassettes. HOW TO WRITE YOUR OWN TICKET WITH GOD was one title available.

As they passed out envelopes for the offering, the pastor quoted Malachi: "Bring ye all the tithes into the storehouse . . . saith the Lord of hosts . . . I will . . . pour you out a blessing, that there shall not be room enough to receive it.

"Shall not have room enough . . .

"The Lord loves a cheerful giver . . ."

Finally Hagin came out—fiftyish, strongly built, six-feet tall, expressionless. His colorful clothes—red shirt and tie, light-blue jacket, dark-blue slacks—were not mod, not dour.

He began talking about the morning teaching sessions and urged his audience, "open your Bibles. We're talking about the tangibility of God's power." The illustrations he used then were all healing illustrations.

"We realize our inability and our insufficiency . . ."

"O yes, Lord," responded some in the audience.

"The more people *know* about the word of God, the easier it is for them to get healed . . ."

Mere laying on of hands won't heal, he told them. In fact, he said, we could lay on hands "till we wore ever' hair off the top of your head" and not get a healing. There was that humor again—that lighthearted, effortless, transparent type of humor that so delights the audience.

40

No ethereal preaching here. Hagin is a quiet bull on the platform. His speech is full, impressive, direct, and it comes across clearly, no vague or indistinct tones, no subtleties, no hidden or inside meanings, no shadings, no innuendos. He doesn't appeal to emotion, but he doesn't quench it. He doesn't shout or scream.

I've never seen a strong man so light on his feet, or so effortless, while bringing peace instead of muscular or mental oppression. He was strong, but he never crossed that mental line to subjugate you. His strength strengthened the audience.

"Jesus used many methods," Hagin went on.

"Most prominent was LAYING ON OF HANDS . . .

"God anointed Jesus . . . in Acts 10: 38 . . . 'with the Holy Ghost and with power' . . .

"Healing comes in obedience with a spiritual law . . . contact and transmission . . ."

He then made a differentiation between the Holy Ghost and the power, stressing that the anointment was with the Holy Ghost *and* with power.

"At Bethesda, Jesus simply said, 'Rise, take up thy bed and walk.' He never touched him . . . Where the man was blind from birth . . . Jesus spit on the ground and made clay of the spittle . . ."

With that marvelous soft humor, Hagin now slipped into a period of reminiscing.

"In my early ministry they brought before me a man on a stretcher. God told me, 'Demonstrate . . . I want you to demonstrate. . . .' Now this man was skin and bones, lying on a stretcher in the last stages of T.B. His doctor said he should be dead.

"The voice said to me, 'You tell the congregation that he'll rise up . . . or tell 'em you're a false prophet."

Smiling, he went on, "He was healed . . . He was healed, and there are several hundred witnesses and five Assembly of God pastors who were there.

41

"I was healed in 1934 when I was seventeen years old. The healing came . . . I was a Southern Baptist . . . and it came reading my grandmother's Methodist Bible.

"The Lord Jesus never claimed to heal anybody . . . My Father in me . . . doeth the works . . . He anointed Jesus with the Holy Ghost and power . . . 'And so God wrought special miracles by the hands of Paul.' "

He then told about Rev. Smith Wigglesworth, a well-known evangelist with a healing ministry in England some time ago. I hadn't heard of Wigglesworth but apparently he was known to that audience. A sick person had sent a handkerchief to Wigglesworth. He returned it "with instructions . . . to lay the handkerchief on the sick one . . . and to start praising God *because she is healed. . . .*"

This individual had ". . . cancer . . . given up by the doctors. . . ." In his smiling, expansive way Hagin said, "They didn't even get to believe."

The thought of everyone standing around ready to believe and praise God and carry out all the instructions coming with the little handkerchief, being suddenly aware that this was made unnecessary by the instantaneous healing, sent everyone into joyful laughter. It was as if the joke was on them.

It was that doctrine again that Hagin was expounding. Man was already saved, forgiven, by Jesus in Jesus' time. By the same token, man was already healed. Man will not be saved *someday* . . . he is *already* saved. Man will not be healed tomorrow, or tonight, but *was* healed, cleansed, made perfect, redeemed, 2000 years ago.

Quite an idea.

". . . By whose stripes ye were healed . . ." I Peter 2: 24.

The absolute dynamics possible to a ministry based on such a concept, if that concept is true, are at once apparent. Sickness can be banished as an outlaw, as an illegitimate thing—yea, as a thing without basis.

Wow! What a concept! It's all set down in Hagin's booklet, HEALING BELONGS TO US.

It was "Jesus' intent" that we be healed.

He spoke now rapidly of a vision or trance he once had in which he went ". . . to the throne of God . . . where He touched the palms of my hands . . . and pressed a coal of fire into each palm . . . and said, 'I have called thee and anointed thee to heal the sick.'"

I could tell by now, by the light and by the change of consciousness, that the experience of the Holy Ghost was close. The pace of the sermon had quickened, and he didn't go into detail in his stories, but hit the "top" of the stories, finding an instant response. The light of some deeper revelation was in the room.

He began to talk about *falling*—the phenomenon of being smitten with the Spirit—and gave biblical references ". . . they fell . . . unusual spell . . . as one dead . . . Paul . . . Peter . . . housetop . . . fell into trance . . . Paul . . . Jerusalem . . . trance . . . physical senses are suspended so you fall . . . three-hour trance . . . She saw Jesus ministering unto her . . . It's in Acts. . . ."

He spoke of "John Wesley, Founder of the Methodist Church . . . in his meetings . . . fall into trances . . . One of these they thought first had fainted. . . ." He was citing now from books. "Wesley himself thought she had fainted and asked, 'Is there a doctor in the house?'" (This brought a big laugh from the audience.) "Said Wesley, 'It's not sickness, her pulse is normal' . . . said an onlooker, 'Is it the Devil?' . . . Wesley said, 'I don't know' . . . Another asked, 'Is it God?' . . . Wesley again said, 'I don't know—we'll wait till she wakes up and whoever it was will get the credit.'

"She awoke. . . . 'PRAISE THE LORD!' she said.

"Whitfield . . . associate of Wesley . . . they were the first two circuit preachers . . . people fell from trees in Boston . . . autobiography of Peter Cartwright . . . Wesleyan Methodist . . . When he preached the power fell . . . people would be *slain* . . ." That's the expression for this trance or stun.

"He was six feet, six inches and wore two inch boots. He absolutely would never dance . . . it was against the religion. . . . He was on the circuit and staying overnight when he was confronted with a situation in which hospitality demanded that he dance . . . the party was in progress, and the hostess asked him to dance, at which he said, 'Ma'am, I never do anything without praying first,' and he said, 'Let's pray . . . God . . . let's save . . .' and people started falling . . . never did have their dance. They all got saved!'

Suddenly, a burst of tongue-talk from Brother Hagin. Like a machine-gun. He was brimming now. The presence was there.

" . . . those who *believe* . . . they shall do exploits in the name of God."

It was a practice of the audience to raise the right arm—even, on occasion, to raise both arms. Face somewhat down, right arm raised—this was a posture many now had assumed. A fifth of the people in the front few rows had their right arms raised much of the time.

The first group of people wanting healing were now in front of the minister. He had let only one section of those wanting healing come forward at a time.

"The Lord told me . . . tell the people exactly what I told you.

"Seven ways or methods of receiving healing. This is only one way . . .

"Say, Lord, I believe . . ." And the congregation said, "Lord, I believe. Hallelujah!"

"Say, Lord, I receive. . . ." And the congregation said, "Lord, I receive."

He stepped down off the platform, then stepped in front of an individual at the far end of the line and placed the palm of his right hand lightly against the forehead of the patient.

The measured tones, "From the top of your head . . . there . . . that'll do it. . . ."

She keeled.

Assistants began covering bodies with towels or coats if dresses were up.

"Satan . . . take your hand off God's property . . .

"Sister . . . receive your healing . . ."

They fell . . . pow . . . they toppled.

"There's your healing right there . . ."

It was nothing for eight to be on the floor out cold.

"Won't do a thing for you if you resist it . . ."

He had touched the forehead of the man who resisted it, and his hand came away almost as fast. He didn't jerk it away; he left it there for a moment, but he came away and moved to the next person.

"EVERYBODY STAND!"

We sang, "Only believe . . . only believe . . . all things are possible . . . only believe . . ."

Three groups of patients had gone through the line and a few were still out cold when he pointed out toward the audience.

"The Lord wants me to minister to . . . a lady with severe back trouble. . . ." The lady came forward.

The lady sat in a chair just left of the speaker's stand, on the auditorium floor in front of the platform. Hagin's back was to me.

Usually in the case of back trouble of this sort, one leg is shorter than the other. He had both feet, shoes still on her feet, in his hands, moving them about in a two-or-three-foot arc so that many could see. Suddenly . . . "Oooooo—Hallelujah . . . see it comin' . . ."

45

He got up off his knees. The lady got up out of the chair smiling. The witnesses seemed satisfied. Another patient sat down in the chair.

Now Hagin was without any witnesses again, and he called for new ones. Up went my hand and he called me. I knelt down beside the lady, praying, but this didn't satisfy Hagin. I wasn't close enough. I wasn't paying close enough attention.

So, Hagin had me come clear around the little old lady and up on the two-foot-elevated platform where I could see exactly what was going on—the chair, lady, and all. She was sidewise, like Whistler's mother, to me on the platform and to the audience from the other side. I was still praying, and Hagin was about to give up on me. He wanted me to *watch that leg.*

Now he—it seemed to me almost impatiently— waved that little lady's two feet around, showing the crowd, but mainly the witnesses and those up close, the difference in the lengths of the legs. He had first caused her to push fully and squarely and flatly back in the chair, which causes whatever difference there is to be apparent.

One leg was plainly one inch shorter than the other, and, holding the two feet together, he showed this to the audience.

Then he rested the two feet in front of him and lightly placed his fingers on the sides of the heels and the sides of the feet and ankles. He was on his knees; her feet were straight out. His face was looking down at the feet with the obvious one inch difference.

Suddenly, there, before my eyes, without any motion of the lady's dress or her body or her knees, without movement of anything that would have had to have moved if Hagin had pulled, which he didn't because his hands did not move, *the lady's legs were equal in length.*

There was simply no movement of anything except

the changing of position of the kneecap and the appearing of the extra length that equalized the extension of the feet.

I believe that in this atmosphere—at that moment—anything could have happened in the way of healing. There was simply that mental atmosphere. I believed, everyone in the audience believed, that this was possible, even normal, even *there* and only needing to be realized.

Do I believe the leg was lengthened? Surely! Could it have been a trick? Surely! But he has published testimonies, backed up by prior medical history (damaged or malformed or incompletely formed spine, connected to unequal legs, that sort of thing) that his ministry in this field is verifiable.

No rest. No breather. This was a session! Started at 7:30; by then it was 9:30.

Next group up there. Or should I say down?

Zap—all the way down the line.

He was talking in tongues.

Then he was down! Pow! Like he'd been hit on the back of the neck. He was on all fours, shaking it off. Rising.

Fifteen were down. Each was touched on the forehead.

Wham! He went down again! Then he got up and smiled.

"I couldn't heal a gnat's wing," he said.

Then everybody was down. There was nobody to touch, and He was standing there smiling.

Another batch.

He called out now . . . "Come quickly if you want it . . . I'm about to quit . . .

". . . lose your anointing when you get tired . . . I'm gettin' tired. . ."

He bowled over ten or more in the windup, the final ones who flocked up to the call.

47

CHAPTER 5

KEN FOREMAN—FAITH TEMPLE'S JOYFUL NOISE

SAN JOSE HOLDS DOWN THE SOUTHERN END of the megalopolis that surrounds San Francisco Bay. I had driven up to hear Ken Foreman of Faith Temple, then learned that he was leaving town. In his place Ken Mann of San Jose would be holding a crusade.

It was Sunday about noon when I found the spacious parking lot of the light-pink concrete-block church, filled with the cars of the faithful. The service was nearly over, but I slipped into the main auditorium and stood with my back to the wall among other standees. According to the usher, Ken Foreman was preaching.

". . . lady . . . there . . . (he pointed into the crowd) . . . had a . . . disc in the back of your neck this morning . . . feel for it . . . the problem is gone . . . I say God preached some light into you this morning . . . I believe God's Word made you whole . . . you . . . had arthritis . . . feel for it . . . it's gone . . . raise your hands . . ." Four, not one, raise hands.

He identified one lady but she didn't come up. Finally another lady came up. "You're not the one," he said with a smile—headlights coming out of those teeth—and touched her. She keeled and two ushers behind caught her.

"I made the devil mad this week . . . he can't hang around Faith Temple because the joy of the Lord is here."

Preacher Foreman looks like Tom Jones. He wears a Tom Jones black hairdo, black pants, white open-neck shirt with long sleeves. He looks twenty-five but declares from the pulpit he is forty.

"Preachers deal with possibilities . . . prophets deal with impossibilities. . . . I'm not satisfied with being a preacher . . . knowing that all things are possible to God. . . ."

Then he spoke of his love for and appreciation of his congregation or audience. He was preparing, he said, to go away for three weeks of preaching, then vacation, then fasting in preparation for his new crusade. This was a sort of farewell address.

There was a youth band on the platform—two trumpets, an electric guitar, set of trap drums. Foreman called for "Peace Like A River," and it began peacefully enough. Then it waxed stronger and livelier until it had worked up into a big jam session.

By that time Foreman had a big receiving line up front. They came up to thank and to share and well-wish and get blessed and commune with that happy spirit. And he was happy. Tremendous smile, tremendous animation, hugs for everybody—a kind of cheek-to-cheek. Women kissed him on the cheek. The band played. He looked directly into the face of each . . . talked directly at them. This was to be his last appearance for three weeks.

I was disappointed but at least, I thought, I can learn something about Kenny Mann. That evening I returned at seven for the 7:30 p.m. meeting.

I took a seat in a large white oak pew with a gold-upholstered seat. Red carpeting graced the floor and high, laminated-wood arches spanned a church-type ceiling. There were no religious symbols anywhere.

At the front, red-carpeted steps led to a raised platform about two-feet high. A pulpit stood in the center. An organ and a big speaker stood on the right beside a set of magnificent red trap drums. On the left was an equally magnificent sparkling set of blue trap drums.

Microphones were everywhere—hand mikes, pulpit mikes, one on the piano, one on the organ, three hanging above the empty area at the back for the choir. Also speakers—some on stage and on top of the roof canopy, twenty feet over the stage.

At seven-thirty they're pouring in. The band begins in earnest . . . jazzy . . . swinging . . . feet tapping . . . hands clapping.

Now the choir comes in like a flood on the rear of the stage, clapping, swinging, in maroon-with-gold-trim robes, three rows of fifteen.

Making all that music is an electric guitar, accordion, piano, organ, three trumpets and two tambourines.

At seven thirty five four ministers make a grand entrance. One wears a bright-red tailored coat with black pants, heels, pink-and-white alternate broad-stripe shirt, and a black-pink-white mottled tie with a huge knot. The second is well-tailored in a combination of modern-with traditional brown jacket, white pants, white belt, white boots with buttons, grey shirt and white tie, age about 30, mustache, thin face and slim physique. The third wears a green everyday business suit and the fourth, the song leader, wears a brown business suit.

"Lives are going to be changed . . . the Kingdom is going to be increased tonight . . . because souls are going to be added. Do you believe it? . . ." Baker, the song leader, is up and working.

Looking out over the audience with an all-knowing smile all this time is the one in the red coat. He looks familiar. In fact, he looks like Foreman. He keeps time to the music, smiles, and finally leaps up.

His favorite song; that's what he wants now. "This Is My Commandment, That Ye Love One Another." Now I'm sure. It is Kenny Foreman, pastor of this church.

"A church should show itself friendly . . . if you've got any bitterness in you . . . any prejudice . . . any animosity . . . God can't dwell in such a heart. . . ."

This is Tom Jones. He's got it—facial expressions and everything.

"I make no apologies for being happy tonight . . . people take tranquilizers, pep-pills . . . pay a psychiatrist $35 an hour . . . I don't have to *find* it . . . I take it *with* me . . .

"God's *EVAH WHARE!* . . ." he shouts, and repeats it several times.

By now I assume that Mann is the slim fellow on the left with the mustache. Foreman must be doing this bit for him as an introduction, but Mann has a "Who can follow this?" look on his face.

Foreman is really steamed up. He hollers, "Worship the Lord with *joy* . . . you get strength . . . you get *newness* . . . and freshness . . . WHOO! . . ." He sticks out his foot and swings around.

"*That's* not my sermon," he declares. "I already preached more than most preachers in a week—*said* more, anyhow . . ."

Danny, the organist, is now at the piano, singing. Foreman is into everything, the center of everything even when sitting in his chair and supposedly leaving the stage to someone else. He's a showman.

Someone from the choir comes forward to sing a solo. "I know my sins are forgiven, and I'm on my way to a place called Heaven . . ."

The background is jazzy and the choir and then the audience join in on repeated choruses.

The audience is on its feet now clapping, tapping seats. Foreman is up, standing behind the singer. Even

51

the staid green-suited preacher is clapping. And my foot is going.

Now Foreman is preaching on noise. "The devil makes every kind of noise there is—'wrassling' matches, football games, baseball games, political conventions . . . it isn't the *noise* the devil minds . . . it's the *kind* of noise . . . joyful noise unto the Lord. . . .

"Give the Lord a clap-offering."

I've never seen anything like this. The crowd approaches ecstasy. The clapping had started out to the music, then moved to the clap-offering to the Lord . . . then died away as if to quit . . . now it comes on again with a vitality from another dimension.

It moves in soft waves over the audience. Most are standing, faces radiant, uplifted, eyes closed, hands raised in that familiar posture. A choir girl gets the Holy Ghost while standing there singing. She raises hands, goes into prolonged talking in tongues.

"Wow!" says Foreman. "Wow . . . You can sit down now if you can. . . ."

A Roman Catholic gets up and testifies to being "in the Lord." He's been in this church one month. Foreman, standing on the audience floor with mike in hand, calls out another person, "precious little mother . . . a Catholic. . . ." He and she talk.

He asks for "that child I prayed for whose eyes were straightened last week." Not there. He calls out "little mother" who comes up, and he lays hands on her eyes, rebukes the "curse of this disease of sugar diabetes," asks God to "heal these eyes . . . and fill her with the joy of the Lord . . . Did you feel something?" he asks. "Yes, I did," she answers.

Now it is offering time. He comes straight to the point about offering. "Sometimes our Sunday night collection is only $200 out of a thousand people. Well, that is not enough for our expenses."

During the announcements I learn that Kenny Mann

52

will preach Wednesday and start his Crusade *next* Sunday night for a week.

Now Foreman sings ". . . Just sit my mansion next door to Jesus. . . ."

He's a show biz personality, a great single. He could go on at Las Vegas.

The singing goes on. The audience is up on their feet—singing, clapping. It's 8:50 p.m.

"I'm gonna preach fifteen minutes now . . . I just feel the presence of the anointing of the Lord tonight. . . ."

He preaches on despair and hope, using illustrations for both Old and New Testaments.

Without any break from the sermon we're into the healing activity. Foreman points out into the crowd. "Sister . . . with that hearing aid . . . will you come up?"

She is about seventy. Ushers stand behind her. "It's never too late . . . no despair . . . there's always hope . . . Jesus has already touched you . . . I'm not going to lay on hands . . . you're healed right now . . .

"I say Jesus has done something for you tonight . . ." Now she's up on the stage and he touches her forehead. Danny plays softly on the organ.

Foreman speaks into her ear while she plugs the other one. "Say, 'Thank You, Jesus' . . ." She does. "Say 'Hallelujah' . . ." She does. "Say, 'I love You, Jesus . . . for healing me' . . ." She does.

Now came a spontaneous outburst from the little lady, who, all of a sudden, lit up like a light bulb and said, with a smile of astonishment and recognition, "And unstopping a stopped-up ear . . . ha ha ha!" Her laugh came on her as she recognized she could hear through that ear.

"You won't need that now," Rev. Foreman refers to her hearing aid.

"I'll just take that to my church," she says, "and I'll

53

tell them what a wonderful God we've got out here."

Foreman, pointing into the audience: "The lady with her hand up . . . white blouse . . . black dress . . . you've been troubled with something with which you've not gotten any help . . . you've been releasin' your faith back there . . . As you walk up here, God's going to grant you a miracle. . . ."

She comes up and he says, "Something's already happened . . . let that Spirit flow . . . let that Holy Spirit flow . . ." He touches her head and she staggers and waves her arms continually. He touches one of her arms and this quiets her.

Now he returns to his audience, pointing, calling out, "I want two people . . . quickly come . . . suffering from deafness in one ear or another . . . all right . . . all four of you . . ."

Four come forward and he starts with a big Negro gentleman, portly, dressed in business suit. "I speak words to you . . . I speak words to you that are spirit and life . . . receive your healing right now in Jesus' name." He keels. Pow! The ushers catch him.

A tall blonde is before him. "I don't even have to pray for you. Something's happened . . ." She is moving her jaw around in wide circles, and she keeps moving it . . . keeps moving it for the next two or three minutes.

"You couldn't move it?"

"I couldn't move it, but I can move it now," and she keeps on moving it while he goes on to another patient.

The portly Negro in the business suit is back on his feet. Foreman goes to him. "Was it total or partial deafness?"

"Partial."

"What's your name?"

"Bridgewater."

"Say, 'Thank You, Jesus.' "

54

Foreman goes farther and farther back from Bridgewater, dropping his voice to a whisper, then to five or six feet, or seven feet, to an inaudible level. But Bridgewater hears him, and booms out the responses, "Hallelujah . . . I love You, Jesus . . . Thank You, Jesus. . . ." and so on. Foreman has him up there for what seems to be several minutes, as he drops farther back, dropping his voice each time, having four or so responses each time, until everyone is satisfied.

"Let's have a big hand for Jesus," Foreman cries and the audience responds wildly.

Now to a big lady, about sixty, in a red dress, he says, "You had a very serious bone disease in both your ears . . . I say, you *had* a very serious bone disease . . ." She is trying to cut in, but he keeps saying, "You *had* . . ." and smiling, in total control. She is on stage. "It's . . . Oooooo! . . . let it flow . . . now . . ." He touches her head and she talks in tongues.

Foreman, smiling, turns to audience and says, "You don't *have* to understand . . . she's talking to God . . . to the Holy Ghost tonight."

The lady then speaks over the mike in Foreman's hand. She cries, "I prayed for *years* (her voice breaking, the tears coming) for my healing . . . but God told me through my husband's mouth the other morning that I would receive laying on of hands and my healing . . . I can hear perfectly . . ."

"Go ahead and shout," says Foreman, and the crowd cheered and stomped.

Foreman: exultantly, "Oh, the devil's a liar and the father of it."

A tall man in a business suit, sixtyish, is up front and Foreman turns to him. "I don't have to pray for you . . . you got your healing when she was rejoicing over hers over there . . . stop up your good ear . . ." And he went through his repeat-after-me, backing-away routine. The man was obviously delighted with what apparently was a healing of deafness.

"I want three people that's been suffering with arthritis—stand to your feet now . . . there's five . . . Mom, where's your arthritis?"

"Hand and back."

"As you walk toward me, something's going to happen."

She's on stage now. "I want you to move your back. Bend over." She does and opens and closes her hands high in air. Foreman, grinning, communicating utterly with everyone in the audience, "And she's not a little *Pentecostal* lady . . . She's . . . Presbyterian."

"Where's yours?"

"Spine."

She comes down front to the floor area on the left, but not on stage. Here Foreman ministers to her. She is fiftyish, wide in the waist, blue dress, matronly, grandmotherly figure.

"I speak the words of Jesus . . . bend over in the name of Jesus . . ."

She bends over so that her hands are about two feet from the floor. Miraculous—this is as far as she'll ever get. It seems impossible that a lady of that weight and size and shape and age could ever bend that far, arthritis or no arthritis.

"Bend over again. . . ."

She straightens, bends again, without interruption, now reaching within about a foot of the floor. The third time she almost touches the floor.

Now she holds arms out and twists her body as though in calisthenics. For a lady of her size and shape, she's doing fine—and the crowd loves it.

The lady says, "I stay in bed all the time. . . . I'm supposed to be in a brace . . . but took it off . . . waitin' for my healing."

Foreman: "Go ahead; bend over."

This time she does it, touches the floor three times then quits.

Foreman turns to another woman and says, "Get your mind on Jesus . . . Get your mind on Jesus . . ." He touches her forehead, and pow, she's down.

Next!

The action is very fast now, and I hear him say to a woman, "Take a little run for Jesus . . ."

He's winding up. Or is he? ". . . something that's worse than cancer . . . worse than cancer . . . and that's separated from God . . . I have no power to save you . . . but I point you to Jesus . . . somebody who loves you . . . more than anybody in the world."

Throughout all this Foreman has been laughing and smiling. Now he gives an altar call.

When I finally left—a good hour after the altar call—there were still forty or fifty people in the church building, and Kenny Foreman was on stage with a group. I saw his hand go up and touch a forehead.

CHAPTER 6

PORTLAND TEMPLE—WINGS OF HEALING

IN PORTLAND, as I often did in a city, I spent an hour or so on the phone, following one lead then another, trying to determine the extent of healing activity in that city. After several conversations with secretaries at various churches, I called the religion editor of the OREGONIAN.

"Let me look at my advertising page," he said. "Last week . . . local temple . . . 'C. A. Scott, Belfast, Ireland . . . Four Great Healing Services' (he was reading the ad) 'Miracle Temple Church' " Then he added something about "special healing for the teeth." Then another, "Lawrence and Marie Vandervort, New Era Spiritualist Camp, nine miles south of Oregon City. N-period-S-period-A-period-C-period . . . whatever that means . . . 'medium and healer' . . . it says."

But it was in the yellow pages that I got my big lead in Portland. "Portland Temple Wings of Healing." A call produced Mrs. Wyatt, the pastor's wife. "We have our Coffee House . . . 7 or 7:30 p.m. till midnight . . . Fridays and Saturday nights . . . young people . . . saved, healed . . . come in the side, under the church."

Mrs. Wyatt gave me more information about healing in Portland, and it was through her that I learned about William Waltz of Miracle Temple.

I called William Waltz and Mrs. Waltz informed me he was in Canada but would be back for the Sunday meeting. ". . . just closed . . . Brother Scott from Ireland . . . . four got teeth healed . . . one had a cross on it . . . no healing service as such now . . . no crusade . . . just come up . . . prayer for the sick . . . as it says, 'call for the elders of the church' . . ."

She was quoting from James 5: 14-16, "Is any sick among you? let him call for the elders of the church; and let them pray over him . . . And the prayer of faith shall save the sick, and the Lord shall raise him up . . . pray one for another, that ye may be healed. The effectual fervent prayer of a righteous man availeth much."

By telephone I talked to an "elder statesman" of the healing movement, Rev. Everett B. Parrott. "I just closed in Atlanta . . . second Easter in a row and invited back for next Easter . . .

"Do you know Kathryn Kuhlman? . . . Do you believe she has a God-ordained ministry . . .?" This latter question was to qualify me. "She grew up in my meetings. . . that's where I met Kathryn and her sister . . . their father was mayor of the town . . . she was a little girl when I first met her. . . . I married the eldest daughter . . . so I'm Kathryn Kuhlman's brother-in-law.

". . . the greatest argument for spiritual healing is just to observe these things . . . you can't defend it by argument. . . ."

He spoke of raising a dying man. "He has had a big church in Colorado . . . name is Rohm . . .

". . . This thing is all over the country . . . Can hardly find a Spirit-filled man who isn't healing . . . Churches aren't doing it . . . They're not going anywhere . . . organized to death . . . entertained to death. . . ."

He reminisced about some of the old-timers. "Dr.

Charles Price . . . he's passed on . . . became one of the greatest . . . Fred Bosworth . . . nobody to that time had greater ministry . . . greatest crowds . . . Bosworth brothers."

I asked about local healing churches and he said ". . . best church in town . . . power and blessing of God on it . . . Iverson . . . on Glison St. . . . Jesus Christ is the answer . . . large attendance . . . wonderful spirit. . . ."

I called the Rev. K. R. Iverson, talked with Mrs. Iverson and noted again the emergent pattern that was different than what I had expected. "Sometimes on Sunday my husband calls for those who need healing to come forward . . . there is prayer at every service for those who are sick. . . ."

My question about healing services was interpreted by all to mean a certain *type* of service, a "special service." Healing, I was learning, was a part of regular services. And part of that scene was the congregation praying together."

I met Dr. Max Wyatt, pastor of Portland Temple Wings of Healing, in his church office. It reflected the man—vitality, energy. A solid wall, some eighteen feet wide and ten tall, was covered with books.

"My father was a Methodist preacher . . . given up to die . . . something in his back . . . Lord came . . . 'I am the Lord that healeth thee' . . . he was healed . . .

"He started preaching healing. The Methodist Church frowned. He had to leave . . . went Pentecostal."

Thomas Wyatt was well-known to many. The son related that the father was saved almost fifty years ago, was ten years a Methodist, then Pentecostal until his passing eight years ago. He had a healing ministry for more than thirty years. He and his son started the Portland Temple, "built the first structure in 1940, rebuilt it twice . . . urban renewal bought it . . . been here ten years."

In Portland they went on the radio for five days a week, fifteen minutes a day, with the "Wings of Healing" program. Father Wyatt enlarged this to a national program on Sundays with son Max preaching one-third of these. The elder Wyatt was on the air twenty-four years nationally, and the program is still aired with Pastor Wyatt's stepmother preaching.

Pastor Wyatt firmly believes you have a "living experience in Christ . . . When a church loses it, then they turn to rituals . . . We experience things in God . . . When we lose the experience, we turn to doctrines . . . I don't need a doctrine of divine healing. I practice it . . . demonstrate it . . . I don't need a doctrine of salvation. I am in salvation . . .

"Healing movements started with the poor . . . In India . . . untouchables had no god . . . gave them Jesus . . . this opens their entire life upward . . . huge crowds . . . we would preach, pray for sick, then appeal for salvation . . . to accept Jesus . . . not an altar call first . . ."

He reached onto the bookshelf and took off a picture of a little girl. "This little girl was paralyzed . . . unconscious . . . four days . . . Her father got her all the way down that aisle, so I had to pray for her right away. It was our second meeting in India . . . sixteen years ago . . . in Kumbanad . . ." (Evidently, Pastor Wyatt, that evening in India, would have preferred holding this case for later.) "I began praying . . . the interpreter said the fever was leaving, and it was . . . She immediately became conscious . . . got up . . . crowd loved that . . ."

Wyatt spoke forcefully, continually and rapidly. The humor was there, and he told his stories as if you were the one experiencing them, not him.

"The Indians wanted the worst cases first . . . one night they brought two insane . . . great crowd that

61

time . . . I was almost scared . . . God instantly put those two in their right minds . . . I told them to take off those chains the next day . . . they were welded into those chains, and it's quite a job to get them off . . . but they did. I had them on the platform next night . . ."

I asked a number of questions about the Holy Ghost and what happens to a person who is "anointed," and Pastor Wyatt rambled for a while.

"I believe that when I have the Holy Spirit and am walking with God, that God gives power to us . . . The Bible says you go heal the sick . . . you lay hands on the sick and they shall recover . . . It's the Lord doing it . . . but it's us, you might say, acting in His stead. . .

"Others may say 'I have no power . . . only the Lord heals,' or 'But Jesus can heal you all' . . . but if they had no power, what are all the people there for? . . . He does nothing without us . . . We are bringing the healing to the people in the name of the Lord . . .

"We believe in Baptism of the Holy Ghost, with evidence of speaking with tongues, and we also believe in divine healing. These things designate you as being Pentecostal.

"I firmly believe that organizational structure has a tendency to stifle the real flow of the Spirit. This has always been the case in great revivals of the past . . . God has a revival to bring men out of a spiritual bondage they get themselves into . . . invariably man turns around and builds the same bondage . . . one is the Spirit . . . one is organization of men.

"A revival has never come to an organized church. It comes to people. If they remain in it, the organization swallows it up and that ends the revival.

"Churches speak in tongues and preach it, but don't call it Pentecostal. Old-line denominations don't want to use the word 'Pentecost' . . . instead of the word 'Pentecost,' they're using the word, *charismatic*."

What of the term, "Spirit-filled believer"? I asked.
"A Spirit-filled believer is the same as a Pentecostal believer," Wyatt answered.

"Pentecost made mistakes in the past. They now—the new people—want the experience and blessings without paying the price of association with the name.

"There are lots of church groups that believe in spiritual healing but have not put it into operation . . . Mormons believe . . . all believe in the Holy Ghost . . . most believe God can heal . . .

"When I was young if you spoke in tongues, you got kicked out of your church . . . you organized a church . . . and there started a Pentecostal church. You can go into any Pentecostal church and ask how many were Catholics, Baptists, Methodists, and get hands.

"Since World War II the organizations have not been putting these people out . . . they've given it new names such as charismatic and glossolalia . . . being filled with the Spirit . . . fullness of the Spirit . . .

"Catholic ecumenical movement got outside their ranks . . . ran into the Spirit moving . . . some got the Spirit . . . Now it's spreading through their ranks. They don't know where it's going to stop."

Pastor Wyatt told me of a magazine on this topic published by Catholics. He produced several copies of the NEW COVENANT magazine from a stack of publications. The July, 1971, copy is the "Special Issue on Fifth International Conference."

At about 8:30 p.m. that Friday night I entered the Rose of Sharon Coffee House in the basement of the Portland Temple Wings of Healing. I went sans tape recorder, sans large black tablet, trying to fit into the sixteen-to-twenty-four age group.

I was concerned that people would recognize an outsider—especially a reporter—and the recognition would destroy the small-gathering intimacy I wanted to experience and report.

From a literature table I picked up a leaflet, "WANTED," with a picture of Jesus. The ceiling was low, the lights not dim, not bright. Six tables surrounded the center floor space where a microphone stood alone. Posters, some hand-painted and lettered, covered the walls. An upright piano stood in a corner and some fifteen young people sat at the tables, talking quietly.

I noticed that this quiet crowd didn't feel they had to make my acquaintance. It was not like some parties where your very presence made people feel they had to come forward and had to say something. I felt completely at ease in this culture. There was friendship here without talking, but it was very relaxed. Almost as if this special informality was the culture.

Entertainment started and everybody focused on what we would have called a "postage stamp" dance floor some years back. But this was the entertainment area. A young couple, both playing guitar, sang and smiled and talked. It was pleasing, gentle, folk music, professional in a casual way, and it was all strictly low key.

The few adults I noticed either stayed in the kitchen or sat on a bench near the back. Soon there were thirty people in the room, plus the musicians.

The first group of songs were current popular songs . . . a few oldies-for-the-young thrown in—hits of several years back. Then there was a shift to Jesus songs, light songs with guitar accompaniment that had religious themes . . . but without force. "The joy of the Lord is my strength . . . O happy day . . . When Jesus washed . . . when he washed . . . when Jesus washed . . . my sins a-way." The audience joined in on the chorus.

I met Stan Smith, 31-year-old director of the coffee house. "I was at a low point . . . divorce, physical problems . . . financial problems . . . mental depression

. . . when I met Jesus at a Christmas service. God gave me the love I've been seeking all my life . . ."

One of Stan's problems had been a bad stomach condition, a medically-diagnosed ulcer. The "doctors wanted to cut it out . . . do their thing on it . . . prayer . . . in seven seconds I was healed . . . could feel God's hands in my stomach moving parts of it around. . . ."

He showed me his recent sprain healing. It had been at the knuckle or joint between the big toe and the foot. He spoke of having rebuked it, then added, with a smile, "Rebuked the devil, not the foot."

Later in the evening when the music was not to my taste, I went into the kitchen for escape. There I drank grape punch, ate cookies, and talked with one Mary Nash—a perfectly white-haired lady, slim, attractive, about sixty, with a bright, clean radiance. You could tell she kept the right thoughts.

She talked about many things. "I've been here twenty-four years," she said.

"They preached divine healing strongly . . . that's what attracted me . . . that there was a God and that He heals . . . Our family has had very few doctor bills. I'd just pray for them and they'd be healed . . . Average family spent $600 a year on doctor bills fifteen or twenty years ago . . . never had those bills . . . wouldn't say all of church is that way but it's just the way I believe . . . if the Spirit of the Lord is dwelling in me, I shouldn't stay sick . . .

" 'Greater is he that is in you, than he that is in the world,' " she quoted from I John 4: 4. ". . . with me it's not just a philosophy. It's a reality!

"The Lord is just as present in the middle of my home with me as in church . . . day and night . . . We've never had any sickness in the family—not even tonsils. . . . The most I've had is a tooth pulled.

"You have to have faith . . . even in a prayer line.

"Anybody who preaches divine healing gets tested

severely because the devil doesn't want it preached. Back of each one of them (the preachers) is a story of near-death."

I could hear witnessing and counseling going on in the next room, so I excused myself from Mrs. Nash and went back. One man was talking about Jesus to another while two more listened. While I listened Stan Smith began to pray for the man, eyes closed, hand on the man's back, audibly praising God, thanking Jesus and rebuking specific devils as he saw them—depression, spirit of ESP, epilepsy and others. He spoke a moment or two, a sentence or two, in tongues.

Then, suddenly, Mrs. Nash appeared behind the man and laid a hand on his back, and I heard a weeping voice with a clear Chinese or Japanese dialect. The weeping voice lasted perhaps thirty seconds, then it was not weeping anymore, but talking fast and clear, in Japanese or Chinese, it seemed to me.

Mrs. Nash was doing the talking—or was it Mrs. Nash? She had her head tilted slightly down, with eyes apparently closed. Her hand remained on the man's back gently. Her voice was above conversational level, but not what you would call loud. It was definite and pronounced. She was very sure of what she was saying.

By the watch, she talked in this clear, perfect, everchanging, never-repeating, never-uncertain, extremely complex, diverse language for over five minutes. Then, just as suddenly, there was Mary Nash, the lady with the cookies, standing, sweetly smiling as if nothing had happened.

CHAPTER 7

SPIRITUAL SEATTLE

AFTER AN HOUR or so on the phone in Seattle, I felt I had a picture of the "healing service" scene in that city. And that was difficult because, for the average church, they didn't exist. The picture took shape the same as it had in other cities. The "healing" churches held meetings three or four times a week but they were not "special healing" meetings. No, they were routine church meetings at which healing took place, because healing is as much a part of the gospel as anything else.

My first Seattle appointment, Pastor Roy Johnson, led me to a spacious, orderly office on the second floor of the Philadelphia church. He might have been the Methodist or Baptist minister. Both the man and the church had an old-line denominational feel.

I sat facing the book shelves and had the same impression of quality, dignity, order. Johnson, in business suit and tie, sat several feet away.

"Is this book going to be derogatory?" he asked, smiling.

Courage here: He would tell his tale even in the face of the critics.

"No!" I assured him I was friendly to healing, but also open, and I would call things as I saw them.

It turned out that a man had interviewed Pastor

Johnson not too long ago, as part of a project that became an article in READER'S DIGEST entitled "Beware of Commercialized Faith Healers."

"Of course there are counterfeits in anything. How would you tell the real? There are quacks in medicine."

"Are you saved?" the pastor wanted to know.

Just then the phone rang and later Johnson told me about the caller. "This man was injured in the eyes . . . a neighbor had blinded the man's dog . . . they had to kill it . . . he complained . . . the neighbor shot acid into the man's eyes . . . there was a criminal conviction . . . won $33,000 in a civil suit . . . in Seattle . . . his eyes were so sensitive that he couldn't see light . . . healed . . . now has 20-20 vision . . . Lloyd Benson is his name . . .

". . . people healed of cancer . . . internal difficulties . . . leukemia . . . what haven't they been healed of?

"We don't hold what you'd call healing services . . . we heal at all services . . . Saturday night prayer for the sick . . . Half the time I pray at the door when I'm shaking hands with them . . . as for healing lines, we might have that but not regularly."

"How long have you had your ministry?"

"I was converted to Christ in 1932.

". . . nearly all . . . all . . . Pentecostal ministers pray for the healing of the sick . . . one of the side benefits of the Gospel . . . healing of the sick . . . older brother is a minister . . . Retired now . . . he prayed for the sick. My mother had tremendous success in healing the sick . . . not only our ministers but our *people* pray for the sick . . . why, it's just as common among us as praying for any other need.

"Mother was healed of a heart attack miraculously when 72 years old. Sixteen years later the doctor gave her a check-up . . . said she had the heart of a sixteen-year-old. She died at 94, not of heart trouble.

"Lloyd Benson was a newcomer . . . when he got here he started listening . . . believing . . . receiving . . . then he got his healing, see?" The relationship of these elements was thus outlined.

On the subject of testimonies, Pastor Johnson presented two sides of a question: "Lots of cases are difficult to prove . . . difficult to diagnose . . . however, on the other side, many cases were thoroughly diagnosed and provable to those outside the experiencing group and the believing group. Mrs. Mayhew was healed of leukemia when she was supposed to be dying the next week . . . Mrs. Gates healed of multiple sclerosis in the last two or three years . . .

"We give all glory to God . . ." (And, here was a surprise.) "We don't affirm to have any gift of healing . . . no miraculous healing . . . only access to God through prayer. . . ."

Johnson, I learned, had been at the Philadelphia Church twenty-five years.

"This is an . . . independent Pentecostal church. There is a Bible School in connection with the Church . . . trains ministers and missionaries . . . young people of all different backgrounds . . . a Catholic or two . . . converted and filled with the Holy Spirit."

"Do they minister from this church?"

"They return to the group they came from . . . Assembly of God . . . Foursquare . . . Open Bible . . ."

"Tell me about these other groups."

"They are . . . alike in faith and church government . . . no elected officers . . . one segment of the Pentecostal revival . . . all the various groups of the Pentecostal church pray for the sick . . . twelve or fourteen major organizations of the Pentecostal revival . . . Church of God . . . Pentecostal Church of God . . . Pentecostal Church of God in North America . . . study the background of the Pentecostal revival . . . people in *all* different churches caught the spirit . . .

they started to testify . . . were forced out of their church in many instances to form little bands of prayer-believing people . . . the Holiness group embraced it . . . became the Pentecostal Holiness Church . . ."

He told also of the Scandinavian connection. "How many people?"

"Around the world, ten, twelve million. In America I suppose a couple of million. Two million may be low.

"In the city there is a Full Gospel Fellowship . . . forty or so Pentecostal churches banded together in Seattle . . . seventy ministers."

"Do *all these* pray for the sick at their services?"

"Oh, yes, all of them."

They keep the lights burning at Philadelphia Church: Wednesday Missionary service, Saturday night prayer meeting, two Sunday morning services and Sunday school, Sunday evening service at seven and "lots of other services" including "healing service every Sunday afternoon at three."

We returned to the topic of quacks for a moment. ". . . some have been arrested and convicted . . . you even have quack medicine . . . but that doesn't do away with the Bible . . . or the thousands of our people who pray for the sick . . . get results. . . ."

Now he spoke of "Catholics galore saved . . . filled with the Spirit . . . Catholic priests . . . Father Fulton of the Blessed Sacrament over in the University section . . . praying for the sick. . . .

"See, when people get filled with the Spirit, God becomes so real to them they begin to ask Him for things . . . there's nothing wrong with that . . . He is our Father. . . ."

He listed some others in the area. "Pastor Denham of the Bethany Presbyterian Church . . . Queen Anne Hill . . . Mrs. Betty Quackenbush . . . she's had real success . . . she's a Presbyterian . . . St. Luke's

Episcopal Church . . . Dennis Bennett . . . they've had miraculous healings. . . .

"There's never been a time in church history when God has not been healing . . . one of the finest books on healing . . . by A. J. Gordon, THE MINISTRY OF HEALING. He was a Baptist minister, a contemporary of D. L. Moody."

Later that day I went to the office of Lloyd Benson, CPA, and heard a very interesting testimony. On Nov. 13, 1967, someone shot acid into the eyes of Benson's dog. When Lloyd complained, he got the same treatment and was blinded to a degree that a government agency said it was "as if he were legally blind." He had extreme and painful sensitivity to light, had "six or seven" pairs of glasses, and was in constant pain.

He received treatment first in the emergency ward of Ballard Hospital by Martin Berkland, M.D. Then he visited an eye clinic where several doctors treated him, including Dr. Johnson, an ophthalmologist. He went to this clinic repeatedly for four years.

Three court trials followed. In the first, a criminal action against the acid-thrower in the Municipal Court of Seattle, the assailant was convicted of "assault with a dangerous weapon."

In the second trial, in Superior Court, Benson won a cash judgment against the assailant for $45,000. The third trial was a rehearing of the case by the Supreme Court of the State of Washington. The Superior Court's decision was upheld and clarified.

"I had extreme photosensitiveness . . . terrible eye pain . . . used big 200-300 watt lamps . . . could work only fifteen to twenty minutes . . . not much demand for blind accountants . . . practice went down to nothing . . . some clients sued for work not done because they heard we had a large suit in and they hoped to get a piece. . . ."

"How did the healing come about?"

"Well, I had accepted the fact that the Lord wanted me to live with blindness for the rest of my life . . . so therefore I said to Him, 'My question is, Lord, how do You want me to earn a living?' . . . I had really given up hope . . . I was really *willing* . . . got to show me how to earn a living . . . that was my prayer . . . time I wasn't working I was praying. . . .

"My father-in-law was in Veterans' Hospital preparing for brain surgery. We had asked a couple of different ministers to come visit with him . . . he was in the hospital two-and-one-half months before brain surgery and . . . no criticism . . . we had asked pastors, but nobody came. The night before the surgery . . . we had waited . . . we had prayed . . . we were believers . . . I made a decision for Jesus Christ as a kid . . . at 8:30 p.m. who should walk through the door but Rev. Roy Johnson to see another person who, it turned out, wasn't even there . . . Let's face it, the Lord put Rev. Johnson there. He went and talked to my wife's dad.

"As a courtesy to Rev. Johnson, she went to two services at Philadelphia Church . . . then she challenged me . . . 'You're scared to go,' she said . . . 'Yeh, those people scare me,' I said . . . 'So you're going to be a coward . . .' she said . . . So I went.

"I went to the Sunday morning service. That was the morning I heard the message in tongues . . . 'And I will heal your eyes.' "

I asked Benson about the circumstances of the message.

"The person giving the message in tongues was in the back row of the balcony of the Philadelphia Church and had no way of knowing I was in the church. The interpretation was by someone on the main floor . . . but was given just to the audience . . . however, I felt it was directly to me . . .

"This was my first visit to a Pentecostal church . . . I

was a Presbyterian . . . not a practicing one . . . a poor Presbyterian. . . ."

"What happened then?"

"I became a regular attendant at Sunday morning services . . . became hungry for the Holy Spirit as time passed . . .

"One of my clients went regularly to the Full Gospel Businessmen's Fellowship meetings. He invited me to go with him. At the last minute he couldn't go, but I felt drawn to the service . . . I didn't know anybody . . . I went alone . . .

"I heard testimonies . . . one man . . . Kodiak Island . . . where no fish are ever found . . . Lord directed him to fish . . . he got a full boat load . . . another man testified to having been recently saved . . . another that in a depression the Lord gave him several churches to build . . .

"The meeting started . . . the quartet sang . . . While they were singing, 'How Great Thou Art . . .' I just felt . . . Something just went through me . . . just like that . . . I said . . . 'OK, Lord, You took that pain away from me' . . . I took a pencil and paper . . . the room was dark . . . I knew the pain was gone but couldn't tell if He'd healed my eyes . . .

"I took out the paper to look at it. It would reflect light . . . I could recognize light in the dark room . . . It was a night service . . . dinner meeting . . . I gave my testimony that night . . .

"I went home . . . wife thought I had really lost my mind finally . . . I had all these glasses of various darknesses . . . without glasses, I took a light bulb . . . a regular light bulb . . . and brought it right up to my eyes . . . to prove I no longer had photosensitivity . . .

"I went to work early the next day, worked all day, worked all that week, and have worked ever since."

I asked more about the healing. "My eyesight is now 20-20."

"Was it 20-20 before?"

"No! Within four to five months after the healing, I had an examination for insurance purposes . . . and they couldn't believe it . . . said I had perfect vision . . . right up to the night I was healed, I was still putting a novocaine solution in my eyes to kill the pain . . .

"My eyeball is now larger than it was before . . . also, when I drive at night in traffic, there's a shield over my eyes . . . lights coming at me are handled as if slanted away . . . there's an extra shield that was not there before . . .

". . . whole thing to us is the Holy Spirit . . . most churches believe in the Holy Spirit but don't recognize the power of the Holy Spirit."

Several more phone calls in Seattle led to Robert Sirico who holds healing services in the Bethany Presbyterian Church. Sirico, a slight, dark-haired, dark-complexioned young man, had started out in youth work with drug addicts. At eleven years old, he had prayed for a dog that had been hit by a car . . . and it was healed.

Sirico mentioned many healings—a hip, neck, trick knee and bone cancer healing, among others.

"I am not the healer." How many times had I heard that statement now? "Miracles first started two to two-and-one-half years ago . . . no special virtue . . . no fasting . . .

"Many get healed in these services, and I don't even know it until later . . . We've had great crowds come to these services.

"At times I become aware in my mind that healing is going on . . . At first I refused to accept that God wanted me in the healing ministry . . . healing is not primarily for the healing of bodies but for the salvation of souls. . . ."

"How did you get started once it became clear what you were to do?"

"I had been holding youth meetings. These just became healing meetings . . .

"The first healing in my ministry died in Yosemite Park, Calif. Miracles then began to happen in an unusual way."

Piece by piece he told me the story of Don. He had been the minister in Don's healing, and they had a friendship which, some time later, ended in a tragedy in Yosemite. He spoke many times about this loss.

It was quite a shock, and he centered his mind on Christ after that. That led him to an inner experience of great depth. "When I died to Robert Sirico, I became alive to Christ . . . so saturated with His power . . . miracles couldn't help but happen."

In November, 1970, he began regular monthly services at Bethany Presbyterian Church. "The first meeting was filled to capacity. Following that the same thing. We used overflow facilities, then opened steeple microphones and let the message blare out . . . We're still hearing from people in their cars who were healed . . .

"I preach twice a month now in the same church . . . sick people come in first . . . wheelchairs . . . oxygen tanks . . . not everyone is healed . . . God is sovereign. He chooses to heal some . . .

"I am really just a spectator. At times I want to just sit down in the audience and watch." How about that for a statement?

He explained that his services were just like Kathryn Kuhlman's. From his description, I gathered that healings occurred in quantity in the audience.

"Seattle . . . one of the most spiritual cities . . . personally, I am a Southern Baptist . . . Kuhlman is the main one . . . My ministry is like hers, in every way . . . the healing services are just like hers . . .

75

"Channel 5, KING television, filmed an entire service of mine. They ran part of it as a news special—revivals in Seattle. Southern Baptist Convention doesn't sponsor me . . . I am a licensed Southern Baptist minister . . .

"I furnish financial statements to the Presbyterian Board. The collections go to the Robert Sirico Foundation. The money that comes in is not taxed . . . I draw a salary . . . I am just on a salary . . . I have a salary of $100 a week . . .

"I'm not just renting the local church . . . The local board and membership believes, approves of what we're doing. They are members of the United Presbyterian Church . . ."

"How old are you, Bob?"

"Twenty years old. Newspapers sensationalize this . . . I hope that the whole country will turn to Jesus Christ . . . healing is only a means to an end. I'd rather see one person come to Christ than 10,000 bodies healed.

"Took to the radio June 1, 1970 . . . we're on at 4:30 a.m. to 5:30 a.m. each day . . . every day . . . a talk show . . . people are healed all over . . . the station is 5000 watts at 1250 AM, but because of the ionosphere we are heard in Auburn, Fresno . . . British Columbia, 500 miles north of Vancouver. . . .

"We're on at 8:30 a.m. every day with an inspirational program . . . fifteen minutes . . . talk and interview with a person who has been healed and had their healing verified by a doctor . . .

"Whenever a healing is claimed in the service, we try to get the name, address, phone number and follow up in two weeks with a doctor . . . some won't cooperate . . . we have X-rays of curved spines, next day healed. . . ."

"Could people writing college theses come to you and could you furnish names?"

"Yes, we could furnish verified data . . . not X-rays free, due to expense, but these could be obtained at the researcher's expense. They're available.

"My services are not emotional . . . atmosphere is spiritual and uplifting . . . happy . . . too many get psychosomatically healed at the other type meetings . . . . At my meetings no swinging from chandeliers . . . or rolling on floors."

He mentioned "spiritual healing services . . . healing classes . . . healing seminars. . . ." There is no doubt in his mind that spiritual healing can be taught. "Perhaps the next decade will see a real revival of . . . gifts. . . ."

To my questioning he responded, "God is an actual Person, not an idea . . . for instance, in the laying on of hands . . . Christ healing is based on the person of Jesus Christ . . . who I believe is God come in the flesh. Spiritism sees Him as a good teacher or prophet . . . not much more."

I asked Sirico if he had written any books.

"No!"

"Would you recommend any?"

"Just the Bible."

One Tuesday evening in Seattle I visited the parish house meeting in St. Luke's Episcopal Church. Mrs. Dennis Bennett, the vicar's wife, had told me on the phone in the afternoon that Dr. Hobart Freeman from Ft. Wayne would be speaking. "Not healing as such," she stressed. "A prayer and praise meeting."

I had done some research and knew that Dennis Bennett had written two chapters in the booklet entitled, EPISCOPALIANS AND THE BAPTISM OF THE HOLY SPIRIT, published by the Full Gospel Businessmen's Fellowship International.

Some 300 people filled the hall. I had a small spiral pad, so as not to be so noticeable, but noticed that others had pads, too. This was a note-taking church.

It was a mixed group I learned through Bennett's questioning—people were there from such diverse places as Naples, Florida, Philippine Islands, Oxford, Miss.

"Anybody here from Seattle, Washington?" (laughter!)

Four or five gospel songs, the foot tapping type, plus a pep talk, preceded the collection. After another song Bennett introduced Dr. Freeman. Freeman, pastor of an independent church, was in Seattle as part of the Outreach for Christ crusade being held at that time.

"God is restoring the ministry to the Body of Christ ... which is you ... restoration of Apostolic faith ... a ministry of restoring faith ... He said it is a prison ministry ... We're in prison ... bound by tradition, doctrine, error ... physically, mentally, spiritually ...

"Faith is not a doctrine, it is the very presence of Christ ... He said, in My name you can lay hands on the sick, and they will recover.

"By His stripes we *were* healed at Calvary ... claim it. Ask for it ... Christians should stop praying about their needs and start claiming their inheritance ... stop begging and pleading God for things He's already provided ...

"I know a medical doctor ... Spirit-filled ... a woman came in for treatment and he gave her this prescription ... and he wrote it out ... that she should say to herself every day, 'I am cleansed of my sins by the blood of Jesus, and I am relieved of this nervous condition by Christ Jesus.' 'That's the prescription,' he said ... Seventy percent of all ills are psychosomatic ... psychosomatic ... the results of a wrong confession ...

"The best insurance I know is Psalm 91 ... faith spends like money ... faith heals like medicine ... a bold confession shakes the average Christian up ...

"I was ready to write a book on Job . . . his boils and pain . . . how to wear it like a crown . . . grace to bear it . . . found that wasn't necessary . . . found it was the wrong approach.

"In Isaiah 53: 3, 4, the Hebrew reads, 'a man . . . acquainted with grief . . . he hath borne our griefs, and carried our sorrows . . .' "

Freeman claimed a translation closer to the original manuscript meaning comes out like this: "He has borne away our diseases, carried away our sins.

"He died for our sicknesses as well as our sins . . . (Mt. 8: 16, 17) . . . it's a sin to limit God. . . ."

According to Freeman a right declaration—in accordance with what Jesus and the Scriptures taught and presently teach—will heal. "When I claimed healing for my heart attack . . . I said to the devil . . . 'You can't do it . . . Jesus bore my diseases . . . at Calvary . . . two people can't bear them . . .' I never suffered more than 60 seconds from a symptom. . . ."

He spoke of his Cadillac and long drives that he takes over the country. He said, "My Father is not in the used-car business . . . He doesn't want us to drive old dilapidated cars that break down three or four times on the way to a meeting so we can all pray and get more spiritual. . . ." (laughter!)

"Haven't spent a dime on medicine since I was saved, and no one in our church has medical treatment. . . ."

CHAPTER 8

RUTH AND WILLIAM WALTZ— NOTHING'S IMPOSSIBLE

ONE CHURCH LED TO ANOTHER. One phone conversation or interview produced another name. Several pastors, plus the religion editor of the OREGONIAN, had mentioned Miracle Temple in Portland. After cruising the neighborhood for awhile, I located the church by the "Revival in Progress" sign over the front door.

William Waltz of Miracle Temple bears the same relationship to organized religion that a test pilot might bear to a housewife pushing her cart into a grocery store for groceries. That is to say—nearly none.

His is religion-of-the-moment—the inspiration, the prayer, the power. You won't find it in a doctrine-book. They write the book as they go along. But it *is* in the Bible.

The Waltz Bible is in tatters. His congregation is almost the same. These are frontiersmen—looks don't matter to them. This is the wagon train.

If you want to mine a little gold, hang in on one of his meetings where he'll flash several nuggets for you in an evening, but don't be surprised if your old, comfortable sense of church takes a few bruises. This is outdoors stuff. It's on the trail.

In the inspirational, spur-of-the-moment Waltz

church, everything is based on the "presence." It has no large following among the well-to-do. In fact it's a threat to any doctrine-based instead of living-Christ-founded church. Thus it is a little on the side of "outcast."

Inside the foyer a small black lad engaged me in conversation. He was the adopted son of William and Ruth Waltz, from the islands, Haiti or thereabouts.

What? I was just in time for collection here, too? "A miraculous miracle offering . . . Father! Release a miracle now!" I miraculously released another dollar.

It's an old church, 400 old theater-type seats that fold up, with black leather and thin padding. Beams grace the high ceiling; stained glass fills the windows; worn carpet covers the floor.

Now Rev. Waltz, in dark blue suit and open-neck shirt, welcomes newcomers. I raise my hand . . . "God's house, God's people."

The meeting is in progress and a young man guitarist and girl are singing, "I'm a Jesus man." Pastor is praying, seated . . . now he is up. We raise hands. "Any congregation that lifts up Jesus. . . ."

Prayer is for "the presence of Je-sus in our presence tonight . . . and anyone who needs a miracle . . . get healing . . . those who need it . . . fresh vision of Je-sus tonight. . . ." This man talks fast. "Thank You for the anointing . . ."

Waltz' sermon took about five minutes to get rolling, then he burst forth into about forty minutes of the fastest preaching I had ever heard. I never heard anyone speak faster and never heard as many Bible things related to one another. Tonight, he preached from "Passover to Pentecost," he said.

At one point the audience repeated audibly a verse Waltz quoted from Exodus: "I am the Lord that healeth thee." No getting around it—healing is not just a New Testament thing. There it is in the second book of the Bible.

Finally he called people to the altar. Arms went up. A black woman on the right spoke in tongues. "Stand up and let me pray for you. Accept Jesus as your Savior." Three stand. Now all stand and sing. "Oh the love of Jesus . . . It washes white as snow . . . There is power in the blood of Je-sus . . . It washes white as snow."

Forty or more people moved forward to the altar and all kept singing. "Power in the blood of Jesus . . . (three times) . . . white as snow." Waltz entered the audience and talked to the converts.

Then it began. Mrs. Waltz joined him and pointed into the audience, "little lady . . . condition of the back and kidney condition . . . grief over daughter . . ."; she's there now, putting hand to head, "Be thou made whole . . . Praise the Lord. . . ."

For a while I couldn't see what was going on, the crowd was so thick up front. Mrs. Waltz spoke in tongues, heads were being touched, conversations going on, quick diagnoses by Mrs. Waltz which apparently were accurate, and healing.

I moved to where I could hear and see. To an elderly lady she said, "In the NAME OF JESUS . . . from the top of your head to the soles of your feet . . . (pause) you have . . . an attack on the bones . . . especially spinal . . . X-rays show it . . ." The lady said, "yes." "And you'll never have it again! IN THE NAME OF JESUS, BE HEALED . . . there's a warm fire moving out over your bones . . ." She told the patients what the trouble was and the patients verified it. No one told her. She told them either before she approached them or after, or after the laying-on of hands had begun.

As I moved about, a circle quickly formed around the Mrs. and the patient. They held their hands up and toward the patient, in a circle, with elbows placed so that I could not get closer than about three feet.

"By the authority of the Holy Ghost," I heard. She had administered to six since I came up close, and she was a dervish, moving fast up the center aisle, back to the front, wherever she felt the need. The seventh was a man, about sixty, and she told him he had an "ulcer, burning, and cataracts . . . Give your all in all to Jesus tonight, and He'll heal you . . ." Some in group laid on hands.

Back on the speaker's stand, mike in her hand, her voice blaring out, she turned directly to me and called, "Sir! Sir! Come down front. Come over here." What could I do? I came.

"This man's going to write a book . . . it will bless many. Not only that, it will go into many lands . . . I see," and she told me then of personal things in my life, and said, "Is that right?" She was on full mike. "You're right," I said. She was.

She then spoke words of healing to another person and predicted the outcome. Next she was on the floor level, off the platform, and touching my forehead. This was the second time that I had been tapped for "the experience."

By 11 p.m. there were only a handful left, and I interviewed Pastor Waltz. He and Mrs. Waltz are co-pastors.

"The Pentecostal movement was among poor people . . . (whereas) Kathryn Kuhlman has Lutherans, Methodists, Roman Catholics. This healing movement today is not just a movement among the poor, ignorant and uneducated," Waltz said, speaking fluently, readily.

He is about 150 pounds of wiry dynamite on about a 5-foot-10-inch frame. Fast wit, indefatigable. Black hair. Age? About 45 or 50.

"It's an experience with the Lord, not a demonina-tion . . . a Lutheran pastor here received it and is teaching it to his congregation . . . Baptists doing the same. First we saw them coming out of the denominations . . . members leaving for Pentecostal churches. Now the reverse is happening . . . Pentecostal thing is moving into the denominations."

He told me of the teeth-healings at the recent C. A. Scott revival. "One had $140 worth of work to be done . . . had it . . . all filled." He talked about healings on his recent trips to India—numerous deaf, some blind, some dumb—and of a lady in Portland who was three years in a wheelchair. Now she walks.

His wife, Ruth, was "Nazarene, too . . . She calls 'em out by name, address and history and they come up and get healed. . . . One time she reached out in the audience and called to a person in the back . . . Cooper . . . Cooper . . . from Oakland . . . You're here because your mother is dying of cancer . . . the lady stood up, talking in tongues . . . glory fell . . . later we got the report that the mother had gotten up off the death-bed . . .

"It's a body ministry," said Waltz.

"Not a grade school . . . it's a University of the Spirit . . .

"It's not what man says, not what this church or that church says; it's what the Holy Spirit says . . . It's led not by man, but by the Holy Spirit. . . ."

I had promised William Waltz that I would visit him when he came to Bellflower, about ten miles from my place in Anaheim. So one Monday night in August I found myself entering a theater-type building with the sign "The Lord's Church" and another one proclaiming, "Continuous Revival."

Ruth Waltz had been preaching for an hour and had just finished her sermon on the Biblical sceptre with the question, "Do you know why the sons of God have not been manifested yet? They have not grabbed the

84

sceptre . . . Oh, golden sceptre of Righteousness, golden Spirit of Righteousness . . ."

It was a great sermon, and, just at the end, strange noises came from the crowd not far behind me. I turned to see two or three persons trying to revive the elderly lady whom I had noticed earlier playing the piano. She had either fainted or passed on. I guessed the latter. Sitting and listening to a good sermon in her favorite church? Who could ask for more?

"Are you all right?" I heard from the platform. Ruth Waltz addressed the little lady, not the people around her. There was no reply.

"In the name of Jesus . . . I speak LIFE into her very heart," Ruth said. "In the name of Jesus!

"See how the devil tries to distract the service? Shut your hands that way in the name of the Lord Jesus Christ." The audience turned and each person brought his hands up about chest height, palms turned toward the little lady.

"We command LIFE into existence . . . upon her body . . . IN THE NAME OF JESUS . . . in the name of Jesus . . . Hallelujah . . . Hallelujah . . . get your hands right now . . . and just glorify God . . . just glorify God . . . this is the devil now . . . and he'd like to just distract the service. Like to tear down the Kingdom of Heaven . . ."

Ruth went on.

"The devil's a liar.

"The devil is a liar.

"*Praise* the Lord!

"*Praise* His wonderful name."

Granny stirred. They were patting her hands and rubbing them. She stirred and sat up and her color returned. Aha, she's going to be alright.

Oops! There she goes. She had slumped back in the seat. This time it seemed even further.

"Take your neighbor's hand and just begin to rejoice," shouted Ruth into the mike.

"Hallelujah . . . pray Heaven down . . . pray Heaven down . . . Hallelujah . . . gloreeeeee to God . . . gloreeee to Jesus . . .

"Get your mind on Jesus . . .

"Hallelujah . . .

"Reach out and take a hold of the Holy Sceptre tonight . . ."

Little old Granny had turned green. She was slumped down so utterly it looked as if there were only her face there in the bottom of that seat. Well, there wasn't any doubt now.

While Ruth and the crowd hallelujahed and cried, friends began to carry Granny out. She was little, and there wasn't much left of her, but there were four carriers.

She was gone completely, but I wasn't distressed. She had lived her life. She must have been eighty-eight if a day—and lively right to the end. Passing on in church in the middle of a sermon? What more could you want?

"Those of you who want to get the Holy Sceptre come down here and we'll lay hands on you tonight!" cried Ruth into the mike, and they came down. About one full third of the audience came rushing down front, some lagging, though, not wanting to miss anything and trying to watch the final scene as they took out poor Granny.

"Receive it in the name of Jesus . . .

"Receive it in the name of Jesus . . ."

This was a gutty little woman preacher. She rolled right into her laying-on-of-hands blessing for those who came forward and kept it up. Talking in tongues. "Receive it in the name of Jesus . . . receive it in the name of Jesus . . ."

Meantime the organ music came up and the attention focused fully on the scene up front, where Ruth continued laying on hands for about five minutes.

"*Rejoice* . . . tonight!

"Let the Holy Sceptre be given to 'em, Jesus . . .

"Let the Holy Ghost fall . . .

"Receive it . . .

"Name of Jesus, be healed!"

The next night I returned and the first person I ran into was Pastor Phillips. "Well," he greeted me, "you know the little Granny? She's all right." I thought, *what*? I wasn't sure we were talking about the same person.

"Yes," he said, "she's the one who plays the piano. She's all right. Sister Waltz went out and got in the car with her last night and drove home with her and she's all right now."

Then he added, "I sure thought she was gone."

"I did, too," I answered.

Who should come down the aisle at that point but Granny herself, lively, and with her natural if-not-more-so colors, bouncing along like a kid with a basket in a berry patch.

She came right up to me and said "hello" with a sweet smile and shook hands. I was overwhelmed. She then shook hands with two more, climbed to the platform and the piano and played away as chipper as you please for fifteen minutes prior to the service.

One man, about thirty-five, was visibly taken and went forward, fell on the carpet and steps near the piano and stayed there for the duration of her playing.

The meeting began and Pastor Phillips thanked God and called on the audience to thank God for this healing of the sister who, he said, we all thought had gone.

CHAPTER 9

A SOUTHERN CALIFORNIA SAMPLING

I HAD THE FEELING I would like Cerullo before I met him. When he appeared on the platform at the Long Beach Auditorium, I knew it. A short man who does not have the "beautiful people" charisma, he has something more real—and you can feel it.

This was the third of an eight-night Spiritual Life Crusade sponsored by twenty-five Long Beach churches. An ad cited, "Noted, Spirit-filled Jewish evangelist," and urged "bring the sick and afflicted. Rev. Cerullo will minister the healing prayers nightly."

The 1,000-seat hall was full when a warm-up man came out and immediately took the offering. It was a straight-forward presentation of the needs. "Lord appeared to Brother Cerullo at thirteen at a Jewish orphanage, converted him . . ." He spoke about coming attractions, about the costs of hiring this hall and the bigger hall they would have for the Thursday meeting. "You can sponsor a night for $200 or half-sponsor for $100; or a day for $100 and $50 for a half. Straight stuff. No frills. But he couldn't resist telling us the Lord would give us stars in our crown when we see Him.

After a solo Cerullo came on. He was all action and liveliness, dominating the center stage, doing all the talking and singing. He was not the featured speaker, he was *the* speaker. It was his crusade.

The main thing about Cerullo is that you love him. Love springs from him.

It is that thirteen-year-old possibly-New-York-or-Philadelphia orphan urchin coming through . . . all-man, all-kid, all-bravura, all-Italian smile . . . at home on a hard-cement sidewalk fronting houses with steps leading to second stories filled with wives and undershirted husbands, kids and grannies, with ashcans under the stoops, roller-skating ten-year-olds and teeners sliding by, and him king of the walk at the age of thirteen.

Cerullo: "We don't look to a man but we look to Jesus . . . Little eight-year-old girl totally blind in one eye . . . born blind . . . eye was perfectly healed . . . how many saw it?" Many hands go up.

"Written testimony . . . Baptist from First Baptist of Long Beach . . . fifteen years no hearing without hearing aids. Just bought a $500 new one last month. Was a dental assistant."

The lady was in the audience and Cerullo asked her where her hearing aid was. She reached down onto the floor into her handbag to get it.

"Take it back to the merchant and tell him a Jew said to give you at least 50 percent" (laughter). "Then bring the money to this meeting for Jesus."

"So many healings," said Cerullo. "So many beautiful Catholics . . . Episcopalians . . . In fact, I think there was even one Pentecostal" (laughter).

This audience was sedate, well dressed, quiet. They raised hands. They were demonstrative at least to that point. They quietly murmured or spoke out, and you heard an occasional "Praise God" or "Hallelujah"—but not loud.

It was also a mixed-age group—grannies and grandpops, children happily hopping around, teenagers, hippie types and middle-aged. Sprinkled in were the badged counselors from different churches.

Briefly, Cerullo spoke of a new anointing for the Apostolic Church. ". . . church was born in apostolic power . . . is soon to be raptured . . . in a greater power . . . something the disciples have never seen . . . a new anointing of divine healing power . . . people say there's nothing new . . . Nothing new? Oh, you'd be surprised . . .

"Did you ever see man reaching out, trying to understand a supernatural God . . . through the five physical senses: touch, taste, see, hear, smell . . . he can't reach God with those . . . faith is not one of man's natural senses. . . ."

Cerullo continued, "The power of positive thinking can't open the eyes of the blind . . . make crippled legs straight, make vertebrae straight . . . make ears to be opened . . ."

Cerullo prophesied that there was something to come that the disciples didn't know. Close to the end of the meeting he said, "The future of the revival movement in the world today lies in the hands of laymen who learn to do the works of God."

After the sermon there was a healing service that lasted about an hour. Actually, as usual in this type meeting, healing is part of the entire proceeding, so that healings are taking place in the audience during the sermon.

Healing lines appeared on stage. A lady testified that a lump in her throat disappeared that night. Another told of a healing of emphysema of twenty-five years' standing, the symptoms vanishing that night. An oldster, a granny, suffering from a broken hip, danced all over the place, kicking in the air.

A group in the audience prayed with throaty sounds and Cerullo called to them, "You that are praying for that person . . . quiet . . . the Holy Spirit is beautiful . . . tender . . . Just open your hearts . . . don't go aggggggg . . . aggggggg . . . that's mostly man, not God."

To someone on stage he said, "Love . . . it's that simple . . . No struggle. . . ."

A young girl, gangling-colt-beautiful at thirteen, had been healed of warped feet while sitting at the meeting. Her mother was with her on the stage. "Her feet were turned in. She came to be healed."

"Did you expect it?" Cerullo asked.

"Yes, I expected it."

"How did you know you were healed?"

She replied, "I looked at them and they were straight."

The mother wept. "It's that simple," Cerullo told them.

Cerullo does not talk in tongues. However, when he gives them a light touch, over they go. The lines were long and the meeting lasted about two hours. When he finished with the people on the platform, that was it. No after-burner effect there.

Plunk in the middle of the Disneyland bar-restaurant-and-entertainment area of Anaheim, in a building designed to be a gigantic theatre-in-the-round, is one of the larger churches of this nation, sprung up like Elijah's cloud, two years ago, into a great outpouring of the latter rain.

Melodyland Christian Center seats 3,500, is fully equipped for sound, for lighting, for automobile parking in an enormous, easily accessible lot, for a bookstore, for gatherings of 300 to 400 in a side room. A huge billboard-sized sign stands directly across from one of Disneyland's entrances.

Melodyland was an entertainment center that flopped. Ralph Wilkerson, pastor, fought the city council for months to get the building. The entertainment district feared the Carrie-Nation-with-an-ax effect on their thriving businesses, and they feared Carrie's little sister, the general-pious-dampening-of-the-spirits effect. They didn't want any preaching in the midst of holiday spenders and night lifers.

Neither do churches pay taxes, and this handsome new property, if managed right, might produce handsome revenues. But after several delays and much airing in the press, the victory rested with the church.

I attended an early Thursday morning meeting at Melodyland Christian Center and found more than 300 attending—with no special speaker or drawing card.

A testifier got up and gave thanks for his healing. He was scheduled for open-heart surgery, and when he didn't show up for an appointment, the doctor thought he'd passed on (laughter). After the healing, the doctor accepted it and it was verified. There was no need for surgery.

Preacher "Mike," Michael Esses, a Jewish rabbi-trained converted Christian, gave his testimony about nearly dying in the hospital from a heart attack. Pastor Ralph had come in and had laid on hands, beginning the recovery. Esses had been preaching the Gospel to the nurses, he said, and one of them came in and said, "In the name of Him-you're-always-talking-about, I command you to stop that hyper-ventilating." "She wouldn't say his name," Esses laughed, and everyone enjoyed this. Mike Esses joked about his Jewishness.

A lay evangelist sang and I thought I could hear that trained-in-Catholic-songs voice coming through. Sure enough, he was a Catholic. He testified of not being able to sing without pain in his throat prior to last November. Then he received Jesus and now sings without pain—"but if I sing a popular song, I get pain" (laughter).

Later, the healing work in center stage began. A woman told about her split-up home being healed after Pastor Wilkerson had told her God had "planted a seed of love in my heart" a few months ago. Recently, she said, the husband had been out of work ninety days and around the house. Wilkerson responded with a big smile that she had really had a healing if she could get along with a husband home for ninety days. That brought a big laugh.

This church heals not on the basis of healing-will-be-available-someday. It heals not on the basis that healing-will-be-bestowed-by-God-today. But it heals on the basis of it-was-won-on-Calvary. It's yours; claim it. "Lord," Wilkerson said, "We accept that healing . . . we believe it's done because of Calvary . . . because of Calvary it's done. . . ."

A public school biology teacher with a gift of healing came to the stage and ministered to a lady with a short leg. She was seated and as many gathered around, they prayed. Wilkerson said, "All of you just praise God . . . Just look to Jesus . . . If something happens it'll be because of Jesus." Then, "They're no longer an inch short . . . Praise the Lord."

The biology teacher had recently had a leg-lengthening healing for a member of his class in school and met with some differences of thought from the school officials. It was a matter not yet settled, I gathered.

Others testified "on drugs five-and-one-half years . . . transformed me . . . desire to be disciple for Jesus . . ." Healing of "small tumor." Healing of "blood sugar . . . anemia," Wilkerson: "You go back to your doctor for verification . . . anything God does can be investigated . . ."

This audience is very sedate, no hallelujahing, no dancing or carrying-on in any way. It's quiet—but it's alive and responsive, praying and in the act. To Wilkerson's light touch, about half of the patients keel.

"Lord, bless this brother that wherever he goes

among those Catholics, they'll not see him, they'll see Jesus. No one can heal but Jesus . . . it's Jesus . . . it's the Lord who's ministering to His body . . . we feel warm toward every church in this area . . . all churches related . . . we're all in the body of Christ . . . people are hungering for God."

Then Wilkerson commented on talking in tongues. "Basis of Jesus is His blood, not tongue-talking . . . tongue-talking is to pray . . . basis is the Lord coming into your life. . . .

"Pat Boone is heading up a group to bring prayer *and* Bible study back into our schools. The headquarters is right here at Melodyland." And, "5:30 p.m. Sunday, the Brother Andrews team, you know, God's Smuggler—they'll be here. But don't come away from your regular church service . . . whatever church you are, be a good Christian. Walk in the Lord."

Melodyland Christian Center was the location of the Fourth Annual Charismatic Clinic, held August 15-23, 1971. The list of speakers at this clinic gives some idea of the scope of the activity nationally. They included:

Chris Pike, Bishop Pike's son, with his conversion testimony and healing of drug-use and an empty life; Rev. Bill Sanders, Baptist pastor of Tulsa Christian Fellowship in Okla.; Rev. Charles Simpson, pastor of Bay View Heights Baptist Church in Mobile, Ala.; Dr. James Pippin, pastor of the 3,500-member First Christian Church of Oklahoma City; Kathryn Kuhlman, author of I BELIEVE IN MIRACLES, and internationally known for her healing ministry for many years; Dave Wilkerson, author of THE CROSS AND THE SWITCHBLADE; Dr. Glenn D. Puder, pastor of the First Presbyterian Church of Bakersfield, Calif.; Dr. Dennis Bennett, Episcopalian rector of St. Luke's Parish in Seattle; Rev. Dick Mills, conference speaker with ministry in the "Word of Knowledge"; Michael Esses, born an orthodox Jew, completed rabbinical training before his conversion; Ann White, author of HEALING ADVENTURE; Dr. Todd Ewald, rector of Holy Innocents' Episcopal Parish in Corte Madera, Calif.; Pastor Ralph Wilkerson, pastor/founder of Melodyland Christian Center in Anaheim, Calif.

The paper of the Melodyland Christian Center talked about the meeting. "The . . . world is being touched by the twentieth-century charismatic renewal . . . Biblically . . . the Baptism of the Holy Spirit . . . imparting . . . gifts not naturally his own . . . qualify him for the service to which God has called him . . .

". . . many who know . . . have felt . . . concern to share the charismatic experience with . . . their denomination. Now . . . Christians from every background are seeking to know HOW to 'walk in the Spirit' . . .

"The purpose of the . . . clinic is to . . . train believers in the Spirit-filled life . . . through . . . Biblical teaching, instructing the spiritually uninitiated, filling in the gaps and assumptions about this experience and by providing further teaching for those who have already been walking in this dimension."

The Full Gospel Business Men's Fellowship International—FGBMFI—is a sign of these times. It reflects the above mentioned aspects and also reveals the United States as the home of many of these streams which flourish and bear thirty, sixty, an hundredfold and much more.

It is non-denominational, thus it is within the mode. It's not a church, but it has doctrine, prayer, healings, saving-of-souls and an abundance of transformed, successful lives. It has more fruit from God than many, if not most, churches.

Demos Shakarian was born in 1913 "into a Pentecostal home and grew up in a Pentecostal church," he says, in "The Shakarian Story," published by FGBMFI. "I cannot remember a time when I did not love God. I cannot remember a time when I did not believe I was a child of God."

He sponsored his first tent meeting in 1940 and the next year met Dr. Charles S. Price, noted healing evangelist. "I found Dr. Price's ministry different . . . My sister, Florence . . . had a collision with a truck carrying . . . hot asphalt . . . she had third degree burns . . . her pelvis had suffered seven fractures, and her leg was torn loose. When . . . reset . . . it was three and a half inches shorter . . . she was compelled to lie in a bed of salve because her burns were so severe that she could not stand the touch of bed clothing.

"X-rays showed that the sharp points of broken bones were headed into vital organs . . . subsequent X-rays . . . showed her condition growing worse . . . if she lived, she would . . . be a cripple.

"In desperation, I called Dr. Price . . . and he agreed to come. It was the seventh day after her accident that Dr. Price reached her. As he prayed for her, God laid his mighty hand upon her body and completely healed her, to the amazement of the doctors and nurses . . . New X-rays were taken, and every bone had gone back into place and the leg restored to its normal length. My sister was able to come home from the hospital . . . completely well . . ."

Those in at the beginning of FGBMFI were successful business leaders and included a tie to Oral Roberts in the person of Lee Braxton. Roberts introduced the officers of the newly-formed organization to his tent audience at Fresno, Calif.

I entered the attractive, modern offices at 836 S. Figueroa St., Los Angeles, and immediately met Gene Zimmerman, chapter and convention coordinator. From him I learned more of the fellowship activities.

VOICE magazine—400,000 circulation monthly;

35 conventions annually; 500 chapters domestically, 200 overseas, an application per working day; 66 international directors; TV in many markets for last two years—half-hour testimony programs hosted by Demos Shakarian. For 1972—one hundred markets with half-hour programs of testimonies.

A chapter holds a minimum of one meeting a month—some once a week. All meetings are open to the public.

Zimmerman told me, "the term businessman may be misleading . . . you don't have to own your business . . . any working man . . . any one trying to make income exceed outgo . . . layman's organization strictly. Ministers can be members but cannot hold office . . .

"We try to keep the meetings . . . not churchy . . . hotel ballrooms, restaurants, cafeterias . . . men only join . . . they won't come to your particular church but they will come to your dinner . . . the manifestation of Spirit they see is love . . . take genuine interest . . . some say never saw such a love . . .

"We have two or three short testimonies—'What Jesus Christ has done in our lives . . . you name it—blindness, leg-lengthening, arms lengthened, cancer." Then he said, "Some are prayed for and die. We don't know why. God is sovereign." As to types of ailments he added, ". . . every ailment healed."

I asked if the organization was Pentecostal. "We're full Gospel," Zimmerman said. "Pentecost today carries only the connotation of speaking in tongues—Day of Pentecost . . . speaking in tongues . . . full Gospel will embrace Pentecost, but Pentecost will not embrace full Gospel . . . most Pentecostal churches are full Gospel as well."

The main speaker at a meeting will be a layman or a denominational minister who has come into the full Gospel message.

FGBMFI have an extensive literature outreach, as evidenced by their snappy new presentations of their famous booklets on the charismatic renewals among Methodist, Presbyterian, Episcopal, Lutheran, Church of Christ, and Catholic. Also in this line are the experiences of attorneys, physicians, and military personnel. They've also published a booklet on the Holy Spirit entitled, STEPS TO THE UPPER ROOM.

FGBMFI, like many in Pentecostal, full Gospel, charismatic groups today, I noticed, is fascinated by the Catholics.

A FGBMFI man told me of an upcoming meeting in which a priest would speak. He was an "educated" man, I was told, and could put things better than perhaps the uneducated. I remembered, though, of another Pentecostal telling me of the unletteredness of much of the early church, and of the speed of the revival through the uneducated and poor.

Today I notice that the revival on these shores cannot get away from this fast enough. The revival has never been as popular—and it has never moved away as fast from the poor and uneducated, nor has it ever moved as fast toward the ancient denominations, particularly the Catholic.

CHAPTER 10

THE ORDER OF ST. LUKE

THE ORDER OF ST. LUKE the Physician is an interdenominational but primarily Episcopalian organization numbering several thousand. It is comprised of laity, clergy, physicians, and nurses who believe all healing is of God, and who feel compelled to make the ministry of Christian healing a regular part of their vocation.

Unlike many facets of the healing movement, we have here a connection to the medical profession. "God uses many agencies for healing. These include medicine, surgery, psychology, and prayer," their literature states. There is also a strong emphasis on the lay ministry.

A statement in SHARING magazine, published by the order from the San Diego office, says it is "a nonmonastic, interdenominational order which believes that healing is an essential part of the teaching and practice of our Lord Jesus Christ, as set forth in the Gospels and in the Acts of the Apostles. They are especially concerned with the records of Saint Luke the Physician and Evangelist. They desire to bring back this teaching to its rightful place within the Christian Church, through constructive teaching and through cooperation with those clergy, physicians and psychologists who have discovered in the Divine Being the source and secret of wholeness. It is comprised of clergy and laity within the Church Universal."

The International Order of Saint Luke The Physician is the outgrowth of the Fellowship of St. Luke, and was founded by the Rev. John Gaynor Banks, D.S.T., and Ethel Tulloch Banks in 1947.

The group's magazine, SHARING, is subtitled, "A Journal of Christian Healing," and contains articles, poems, announcements, advertisements, notices of books, study courses, etc.—all about healing.

A number of the members of OSL have written books on healing, including: Emily Gardiner Neal, A REPORTER FINDS GOD THROUGH SPIRITUAL HEALING and GOD CAN HEAL YOU NOW; Albert E. Cliffe, LET GO AND LET GOD; Anne S. White, HEALING ADVENTURE.

It appears that there are several charismatic movements within the Episcopalian church. The OSL claims that glossolalia is not a part of their order. Dennis Bennett from the Episcopal Church in Seattle is not a member. Hobart Freeman, who had spoken at Dennis Bennett's church had said, "Haven't spent a dime on medicine since I was saved, and no one in our church has medical treatment."

Mrs. Emmett Dally of Buena Park, Calif., told me of the internationality of the organization and the inclusion of MD's and nurses. "Healing is sacramental . . . also laying of hands . . . also anointing with oil . . . these from the Book of Acts. The OSL can include anybody who ministers mentally, physically . . . I'm a member. I had cancer. I've been healed nine years now." When she told me of her healing, she described two surgical operations.

"When you join this Order of St. Luke, you . . . minister to people . . . pray over the sick . . . lay your hands upon them. . . . The basis is in James 5: 14."

Mrs. Dally's vocation in the Order of St. Luke is to

see that churches get healing services instituted. Wherever she goes, she asks, "Do you have a midweek healing service?"

Agnes Sanford has a ministry of healing extremely well-known within the circles in which she travels, but not w·ll-known to the general public. She is an author, but in her own way, she does not sensationally publicize herself.

In my research for this book, I had written the various major denominations and inquired about activities in the healing field. One such letter was to the United Presbyterian Church in Philadelphia.

I received a reply that a special committee on Christian Faith and Health had been active some years back and that a Rev. Paul C. Warren had chaired it. Rev. Warren promptly answered my inquiry that it had been eleven years since the Committee on the Relation of Christian Faith and Health had made its report. He knew some pastors held healing services, and he referred me to one in New York.

I wrote to him—a Dr. Joseph P. Bishop of Rye, and he answered. We hold healing services, "monthly . . . on the first Sunday night . . . October through June. A number of our people are active in the Order of St Luke . . ." He also mentioned that Agnes Sanford would be conducting a three-day healing mission in his church soon.

Emily Neal's GOD CAN HEAL YOU NOW has a chapter on Agnes Sanford. Mrs. Sanford wrote to me that "the best source of information about my work is in my own books. THE HEALING LIGHT, published in 1947, is still considered by many to be the standard work on Christian healing."

A printed list of her books shows twelve major works, which include THE HEALING LIGHT, THE HEALING GIFTS OF THE SPIRIT and THE HEALING POWER OF THE BIBLE.

While most seem to believe that spiritual healing is a gift, some feel it can also be taught. With her husband, the Rev. Edgar L. Sanford, she founded the School of Pastoral Care to "further interest and provide instruction in the ministry of Christian healing."

In 1971 there were ten Schools of Pastoral Care held, four in Massachusetts and the others in California, Tennessee, Michigan, and England. Sessions are generally "open to clergy and others engaged full-time in the healing arts," and attendance averaged forty in 1971.

The Reverend Thomas Roy Parsons, M.B.E., R.A.F., Rector of Saint Martin's Church, London, Trustee and Honorable Chaplain of the London Healing Mission and Chaplain to the Knights of the Round Table, was speaking at the tidy little jewel of an Episcopal Church, St. James, at Newport Beach, Calif.

About seventy-five people attended the service. At one point there was about ten minutes of silent prayer, during which people called out the names of persons they wished prayer for. Some would mention the illness or problem.

"Brought up as an evangelical," said Rev. Parsons, who appeared in his fifties and wore a blue clerical robe with a white clerical collar. "Saw temples all over the world . . . eighteen and one-half years in Royal Air Force as a chaplain . . . had a little church built by Wren . . . knew Michael Harper and Dennis Bennett . . . seven or eight years ago the Holy Spirit transformed my ministry . . . I preach deliverance . . . liberty . . . (Luke 4: 18) . . .

"They shall cast out demons . . . yes, the Lord believed in devils . . . . one of the cleverest things people do today is make you believe he doesn't exist. The great Satan, the great Beelzebub, walking around . . . Jesus said 'I saw Satan' (Luke 10: 18) . . . Oh, yes, he was real to Jesus . . . he must be real to you if you call yourself Christians."

He told about the London Healing Mission. After he started his healing services there, he said he had a flow of people "grateful that there was one church in London . . . they preached to the depressed . . . oppressed . . . possessed."

He expressed gratitude for his "theological training . . . I can tell what's Biblical . . . there's so much rot . . . Jesus is perfect love . . . and He casteth out fear . . . fear that inhibits . . . frustrates . . . makes us go backwards not forwards . . .

"So many orders I can't count them . . . Guild of Health, Homes of Healing . . . Order of St. Luke . . . We should obey the command to 'heal the sick' . . . we should do what we're told . . ."

He offered a tidbit about the Roman Catholic Church, "In the ritual you now can anoint for life and health, not just for death." He said the church in early times began to admire holy men, placed healing into the hands of holy people. And that that's where they lost it.

"So many channels of healing . . . Lord's Supper . . . Do you go to the Lord's Supper? If you don't, you don't love Jesus. He said, 'Do this in remembrance of me' . . . You cannot call yourself a Christian . . .

"Jesus is the healer . . . 'Send me ten dollars and I will heal you'—blasphemous," said the good rector. But I noticed I was requested to put a little in the pot that night.

The causes of sin and sickness are "world, flesh, devil," he said. "The bomb causes leukemia . . .

"Come to the Healer and Deliverer . . . Come to His ministers, His stewards . . . we'll have an altar call . . . then to our inevitable cup of coffee . . . and tea, I hope. . . ."

The altar call was attended by thirty or thirty-five persons, who went up into the chancel beyond the speaker's stand. I didn't go. There was laying-on-of-hands and quiet prayer. No tongue-talking. Everything was quiet and dignified. This took about an hour, after which we did go to our "inevitable cup of coffee" and pleasant fellowship in an adjoining area.

CHAPTER 11

POT POURRI OF HEALING

THE HEALING MOVEMENT has grown beyond the scope
of a single piece of reporting, and while I covered
thousands of miles, including forays into the "healing
centers" of the country, this remains but a sampling
of the scene.

The most difficult to uncover were the scenes
within the well-known denominations where healing is
practiced. I noticed a reticence on the part of most of
these churches to identify healing as part of their
ministry. They like to work on, out of the spotlight of
the world but within the range of the glow of their
own efforts. The prominent or "spear-point" ministries such as Kathryn Kuhlman or Don Stewart are
like the tip of the iceberg above the water. Beneath
the surface there is much more.

From the Oral Roberts folks in Tulsa I learned
about T. L. Osborne and his organization. Their headquarters was not hard to find.

The imposing T. L. Osborne WORLDITORIUM,
fronting at least 400 impressive feet along a major
Tulsa highway, was temporarily closed for summer
renovations. I was admitted, however, to the back and
greeted by a lovely young lady receptionist.

"This is my card. I'm doing a book on spiritual
healing. Your man is a healer, isn't he?"

"Well, the Lord is the healer," she replied.

"Does it work?" I asked.

"Yes," she said, and, somewhat discomfited, left to get someone to help me.

I was directed to a nearby seat and asked to wait a few minutes. I was in the back, in the office portion of a very large building, the front of which was given over to exhibits of some sort for which there were usually tours. The office was enormous, stretching 150 to 200 feet in each direction from me and filled with secretaries and machines.

After a few minutes I was joined by C. C. Grant, editor of the magazine.

"What about healing?" I asked.

Grant handed me a copy of T. L. Osborne's HEALING FROM CHRIST—translated in fifty languages. "Was Rev. Osborne here in Tulsa?"

"No! He is on a mission."

"Reverend Osborne says it is the Person of Christ . . . no doctrine or theorizing . . . definitely an experience of physical healing in Christ . . . Christ the Savior . . ."

As he showed me around, I stayed with our healing theme, and here is where I began to wake up to something I had not known before.

Healing fifteen years before was a tent phenomenon. People didn't believe. Today there has been a massive shift of thought. It was embodied in C. C. Grant's patient reply. "Well, it's full Gospel. Full Gospel includes healing . . . resident in Christ. . . ."

In other words, it has been accepted by these churches at least, and by their constituents and missionaries and whatever, that healing belongs, that it is a part of Christ and a part of what is to be expected from Christ and is thus a part of church today.

I wondered if the old-line established churches have changed as radically as these evangelical associations.

They're certainly not what they were fifteen years ago. They've grown enormously in membership, support, wealth, and activity—and I mean activity. No middle-class, stuffy memberships these. These are rawboned, stripped-down, 100 percent Christian activists out there doing their Christianity in the marketplace of human need and redemption. Where the need is, there they are—not with soup kitchens alone, not with bread alone . . . and this might be the reason for the staggering growth, substance, stability and solidity that has been added to these organizations in very recent years.

Contrast this headlong growth and change from the flimsy-appearing tent-image to the definitely established and permanently housed well-funded churchdom, with the severe struggle of conventional old-line churches to hold their members, their growth-pattern, their ministers or priests and their enrollments in seminaries.

In a little pamphlet, "Light To All the World," you'll learn that T. L. Osborne leads the Osborne Foundation, whose ministry he feels is to the presently unchurched masses. He goes predominately where there are masses to whom the Gospel has not been preached.

All the work is for the benefit of some one hundred church organizations, largely of the "fundamental, Bible-believing . . . old-line groups," C. C. Grant told me.

From the pamphlet again: "It underwrites mass evangelistic campaigns on a world-wide basis . . . Sponsors thousands of . . . fulltime missionaries . . . Establishes hundreds of new churches each year in the . . . unenlightened areas of the world . . . Gives hundreds of unevangelized tribes and territories their first opportunity to hear the Gospel . . . Publishes hundreds of tons (sic) of Gospel literature annually in over 100 languages . . . Produces thousands of missionary films and gospel tapes in over fifty major languages."

I asked Grant again about healing.

"It's in Isaiah 53 . . . 'believed our report' . . . healing is in that report . . . full report of good news . . . *people find that Christ includes healing as well as saving. . . .*"

The evangelistic healing movement has broken out astonishingly from stuttering temporary appearances to bursting permanence. In the last fifteen years, not just a few healers who rocked the world, but the lesser ministers, have come to accept that *healing* is: a) in the Scriptures; b) present, possible, practicable, normal, regular, today; c) part of the "full Gospel" and hence part of Christianity today.

Not only that but the congregations and followers and supporters of these ministers believe the same thing. Growth has come—and it has been sudden—because healing has burst through and, in the last fifteen years, become an inextinguishable part of the practice of Christianity. I don't believe Churchdom will ever recover. It will never go back.

As I researched this book I uncovered dozens of names and gathered information on enough of them to give a sampling here. I wasn't able to visit the following, but I've noted them here to give both depth and balance to the picture.

World Missions, directed by evangelist David Terrell, conducts a radio ministry and publishes a free magazine, THE ENDTIME MESSENGER (P. O. Box 24496, Dallas, Tex. 75224). The World Missions Church is affiliated with the Full Gospel Fellowship of Churches and Ministers, International of Dallas.

Terrell is reputed to have an excellent healing ministry and apparently conducts quite a large portion of his work in the United States (some ministries reported elsewhere are 100 percent overseas). Photos in the December, 1971, issue of THE ENDTIME MESSENGER show a number of healings in the U.S. He has a ministry of prophecy and a large number of tapes available.

R. V. Bosworth directs World Outreach, Inc., headquartered in Dallas (Box 4402, Zip 75208). A letter to him brought a response from a volunteer worker stating that Mr. Bosworth resides in Rhodesia and can be contacted by writing Box 3466, Salisbury, Rhodesia. On the letterhead appears, "Who forgiveth all thine iniquities; who healeth all thy diseases" (Psalm 103: 3).

The evangelistic team of M. A. and Jane Collins Daoud have an important overseas ministry. They publish a small magazine, MIRACLES AND MISSIONS DIGEST, and Mrs. Daoud has a book, MIRACLES AND MISSIONS AND WORLD-WIDE EVANGELISM (1953, $1.50). Headquarters of the Daoud World-Wide Salvation and Healing Revivals is P. O. Box 5646, Dallas, Texas, 75222.

Leroy Jenkins has a spear-point healing ministry of considerable reknown. His book is HOW I MET THE MASTER. Write Leroy Jenkins Evangelistic Association, Inc., P. O. Box F, Delaware, Ohio, 43015. He also has offices at P. O. Box 15577, Tampa, Fla., 33614. Religion will never be the same again to you after reading this book. Another volume from his shelves is HOW YOU CAN RECEIVE YOUR HEALING, also by Jenkins and full of testimonies.

William Caldwell has Tulsa (5356 East 21st St., Zip 74114) as his home base, but preaches extensively overseas with a healing and evangelistic ministry. He has an excellent book on healing, MEET THE HEALER (96 pp., $1.00), full of testimonies. His book, FRONT LINE EVANGELISM, and newsletter of the same title tell in detail of the overseas ministry and include photos and testimonies. His itinerary for fall, 1971, showed Detroit (Ferndale), Youngstown, Oklahoma City, other U.S. locations, indicating at least that part the scope of his effort.

Many of his testimonies have to do with eyes—healings of blindness and one of crossed eyes. THE PENTECOSTAL EVANGEL has "verified and published scores of testimonies of healings which have taken place in our services," Caldwell reported in a letter to me. One of these is described in a tract. The girl's eyes were crossed for seventeen years, wore glasses . . . medically verifiable . . . was a news feature in a newspaper. Her vision is now 20/20, and the restriction regarding eyeglasses was removed from her driver's license. "I was born with crossed eyes. My eyes were so weak I began wearing glasses when I was two. Today . . . I can see perfectly . . . the miracle . . . occurred at a tent revival with Evangelist William Caldwell of Tulsa. During the meetings the Lord made a verse of Scripture very real to me: 'Whether is easier, to say, Thy sins be forgiven thee; or to say, Rise up and walk?' (Luke 5: 23). I accepted this to mean that it would be just as easy for the Lord to heal me as it had been for Him to save me.

"I asked the evangelist to pray for me. He laid his hands on my eyes and prayed. Instantly my crossed eyes became perfectly straight, and for the first time in seventeen years I could see without wearing glasses."

One of the newest names in healing is Roxanne Brant. THE EVENING NEWS, Harrisburg, Pa., April 15, 1971, reported, ". . . 28-year-old evangelist . . . involved in healing since last August 5th . . . 'I was relaxing . . . and suddenly felt the Lord's presence. . . . I saw the Lord in front of me with blood on His side and on His feet and He said that healing would begin that night . . .' " It did.

She holds Kuhlman-type meetings and knows healing is going on throughout the audience. One healing, following her announcement that there would be cures of the mouth in a meeting, was a repositioning of teeth that were badly out of line.

Miss Brant comes from a well-to-do family, attended Dana Hall School, and is a top-flight concert pianist who soloed at Carnegie Hall with Arthur Fiedler and the Boston Symphony Orchestra." She holds a degree from University of Colorado and graduated from Gordon Divinity School, Wenham, Mass., in 1968. She heads the "Outreach For Christ Foundation" of Darien, Conn., whose coordinator is Jack Stewart, P. O. Box 17567, Orlando, Fla., 32810.

POSTSCRIPT

So now you have it—a portion of the healing scene as I've seen it. And as I've compared the past with the present, I've noted this progression—a prophecy, a pin-prick of light, a few converts, then more, then a flowing river, a movement.

So often, it seems to me, this is the record of a religion or a revival. Then something happens. Its place in time expires. Its yesterday's usefulness becomes today's obsolescence. It endoctrinalizes, cans, and puts on a shelf that which was un-cannable light to begin with. Or it is persecuted out of existence. Or the new generations on whom its continuance depends are not the good soil or are not at the degree of man's extremity conducive to the deep reception and transformation and dedication necessary for continuance. Or the revival turns with gratitude to the stability, acceptability, and assets of established churchdom.

Today, I believe, we are witnessing something never seen before. Not one revival, not one stream, not one flowing river, not one movement, but a dozen—all going at once, all claiming God-anointed beginnings, spurts of profound growth and influence and enlargements of the place of their tents (Isa. 54: 2).

I wonder, has the water burst from many rocks at once? Are there streams plural in the desert (Isa. 35: 6)? Is the Spirit being outpoured in many places in this latter time, falling like seed in many places at once (Mt. 13: 3-8, 18-23)?

I suspect that never before has there been a multiplicity of streams flowing with such healing, such abundance, and such transformative power. This may be the difference between today's revivals and those of the past. Never before, perhaps, has healing so definitely broken through. I believe that the healing scene, as we see it in our land today, is profoundly different from anything we've ever seen before.